What readers are saying

"Typically, I've only focused on one type of output from Flare—help systems. Using this book, however, I would be well equipped to try other output formats since the detail given in the book leaves no room for guesswork or error. When you are under pressure of deadlines, this book is the helping hand you need!"

> — *Brian Laing, Documentation and Training Analyst,*
> *Xerox Corporation*

"This book is incredible! It's designed for new users in a way to help them get a handle on how to use Flare and does so quickly with just enough detail. If you're new to Flare, you'll want to read this book. If you've used Flare for a long time, keep this book on your bookshelf as a quick reference."

> — *Deb McNally, Technical Communications Specialist*
> *Dover, NH*

"The hardest part about learning Flare is figuring out where to start. It's overwhelming! This book is a wonderful guide through the maze of Flare features."

> — *Cheryl Landes, Tabby Cat Communications, Seattle WA*

"This book is packed with useful information! The Tips and Best Practices offer great advice for both new and experienced users. It not only provides a logical and easy-to-understand approach to using Flare but also includes useful advice for structuring and developing online help in general."

> — *Liz Lukaszewski, Sr. Technical Communications Specialist*

"I wish I could have tapped into the advice on multi-level numbered lists when I began using Flare—plus the appendix on building context-sensitive help is terrific. This information would have saved me hours."

— *Doug Eaton, Technical Publications Lead, Sensis Corporation*

"This book hits the sweet spot for me. It's exactly what I need to get jump-started using Flare!"

— *Jeff O'Gorman, Specifications Writer, InterSpec*

"I have been using MadCap Flare for two years and although I taught myself to use it by jumping right in, I would have loved to have a how-to book like this one to get started. The application is so robust and full of powerful features, it's a daunting task to get started without additional explanations and best practice recommendations, both of which are available in this book."

— *Melissa Hatanaka, Technical Writer*

"The authors wisely decided to approach the method of creating non-linear topic-based content by using a decidedly linear tutorial approach based on typical workflow. Kudos to them for that!"

— *Colin Walters, Principal Technical Writer, Nashua, NH*

"I consider this book to be really useful for those who are creating their first projects, particularly for those who are new to developing help content and have never used a topic-based authoring tool like Flare."

— *Anna Kuleshova, Technical Writer, Edifecs, Inc.*

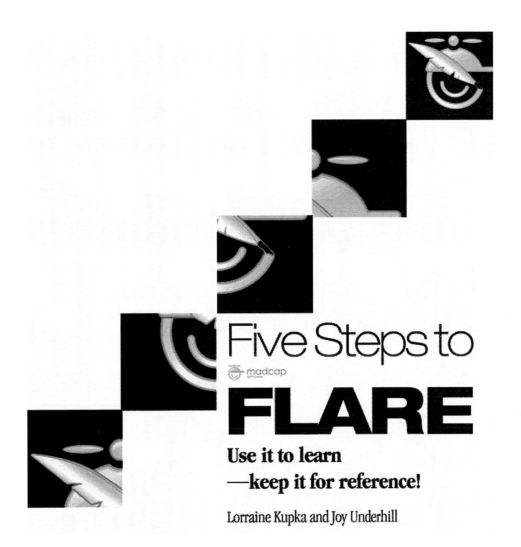

Five Steps to

madcap

FLARE

Use it to learn
—keep it for reference!

Lorraine Kupka and Joy Underhill

WME Books

a division of
Windsor Media Enterprises, LLC

Rochester, New York
USA

Five Steps to MadCap Flare™

Warranty and Disclaimer

Publisher

WME Books, a division of Windsor Media Enterprises, LLC
Rochester, New York, USA

Ordering: www.WMEBooks.com as well as other booksellers and distributors worldwide.

For information about discounts, bulk and special orders, contact info@wmebooks.com or call toll-free 1-877-947-BOOK (2665).

Foreword

By Anthony Olivier, CEO of MadCap Software

We developed MadCap Flare in part because we believe that good documentation shouldn't be hard—and it all begins with content management. To that end, Flare uses a native XML architecture that enables you to reuse content and publish in online, desktop and print formats.

Five Steps to MadCap Flare is a great resource, especially if you're new to Flare and topic-based authoring. It uses a step-by-step approach to unravel the complexities—and flexibility—of the user interface so that you can determine how best to use the product in your environment.

At MadCap Software™, we liken learning Flare to "peeling back the layers of an onion." This book helps you take the first step and realize success with an initial project so that you're ready to take on more. Best of all, it describes the concepts behind the procedures and many of the interdependencies that are not always obvious to new users.

Acknowledgements

Cover design and business graphics: Cindy Harris, Harris Studios, Inc. (www.HarrisStudios.com).

A heartfelt thank you to Nita Beck at Nita Beck Communications for her involvement early in the project.

Mary Anne Brugnoni of Brugnoni Design for her assistance. (www.brugnonidesign.com).

We are especially grateful to our families for their encouragement and patience as we spent many evenings and weekends writing this book or getting caught up on other work projects that couldn't slide.

Contents

Step 1: Get Started 31

Step 2: Learn the XML Editor 65

Step 5A: Create Print Output 179

Step 5B: Create Online Output 229

Appendix A: Planning Worksheets...............................249

Appendix B: Import Content 257

Appendix C: XML Editor Reference.................. 289

Appendix D: Context-Sensitive Help 303

Introduction

In this chapter ...
> Why we wrote this book
> Who this book is for
> What this book discusses
> What this book does not discuss
> How this book is organized
> A step-by-step approach
> Got feedback?

WHY WE WROTE THIS BOOK

We wrote this book because we needed it when we were learning Flare!

We have found Flare to be a progressive and powerful authoring tool, but one with a steep learning curve. Although the Flare Help system is extensive, we wanted a book that would tell us how to get started so that we would be comfortable exploring more on our own.

But when we looked in bookstores, there was no such book. So we wrote one!

WHO THIS BOOK IS FOR

This book is intended for new and experienced Flare users. If you've never used Flare, this book will get you through the basics. If you're an experienced Flare user, this book will help expand your knowledge of Flare and refresh your memory when needed. Our best practices are helpful for both new and seasoned users.

Our hope is that by stepping through this book, you'll be able to successfully plan for and create a Flare project. It won't have all the bells and whistles that you can create with Flare, but it will produce clean online or print output.

Once you've mastered the Flare user interface—and have a good idea of how to build a project using Flare—you'll be able to learn more as you use Flare to create more complex projects.

Flare is like an onion. You learn it by peeling back layers one a time as you gain experience. Our goal is to help you peel back that first layer—without any tears!

WHAT THIS BOOK DISCUSSES

Five Steps to MadCap Flare describes how to get started using Flare. You will learn how to:

- Plan for a Flare project

- Create projects and topics

- Develop content

- Use features for navigating in output (Table of Contents, links, cross-references, indexes)

- Create context-sensitive help

- Use Flare features for reusing content ("single-sourcing")

- Create targets for both online and print output

- Build and distribute your output

This book also provides details about many useful features, such as importing content and troubleshooting your project.

WHAT THIS BOOK DOES NOT DISCUSS

This book does not contain comprehensive information about Flare. The extensive documentation provided by the Flare Help system provides a wealth of information, and we encourage you to use it frequently. (Throughout this book, we tell you where to find specific topics in Flare's Help.)

Our intent is to give you enough information to familiarize you with basic Flare concepts and procedures, become comfortable using the user interface, and create a basic project.

HOW THIS BOOK IS ORGANIZED

This book contains the following chapters:

- **Document Basics** — Provides an overview of topic-based authoring and the types of documents Flare can be used to create.

- **A Quick Tour** — Explains the primary components of the Flare user interface.

- **Step 1**: **Get Started** — Details how to plan a Flare project and complete the plan using a task roadmap. This chapter also explains common tasks you'll do for Flare projects.

- **Step 2: Learn the XML Editor** — Provides a step-by-step tutorial for using common features of the XML Editor and includes supplemental information.

- **Step 3: Develop Content** — Outlines how to create lists and tables, and insert images, symbols, and special characters into your content—plus how to format your content with and without styles.

- **Step 4: Create Navigation Aids** — Describes how to include features, such as links, Tables of Contents, indexes, and cross-references, that let users navigate in output.

- **Step 5A: Create Print Output** — Details how to create simple print output and provides a tutorial for creating more complex print output. This chapter also describes how to build and distribute print output and use page layouts.

- **Step 5B: Create Online Output** — Describes how to create and distribute online output (Help systems and knowledge bases).

- **Appendix A: Planning Worksheets** — Provides worksheets for planning your project and tracking multiple targets.

- **Appendix B: Import Content** — Explains how to import content from Microsoft® Office Word, Adobe® FrameMaker® , and HTML files.

- **Appendix C: XML Editor Reference** — Provides supplemental reference information about the XML Editor.

- **Appendix D: Context-Sensitive Help** — Describes how to create context-sensitive help.

- **Appendix E: Troubleshoot** — Details how to troubleshoot your project and use the internal analyzer provided with Flare.

- **Appendix F: Single-Sourcing** — Explains Flare's features for reusing content from a single source, including how to use condition tags to create customized output, and how to create and insert snippets and variables.

- **Appendix G: The Next Step** — Lists some of the Flare features you might explore on your own after completing your first project.

This book also contains an index.

A STEP-BY-STEP APPROACH

This book is organized sequentially, meaning you should start at the beginning and proceed forward. Once you are more familiar with Flare, you can use the Table of Contents and index to jog your memory about certain features.

How you will use this book depends on your experience. We recommend that:

- **If you haven't used a topic-based authoring tool**, read the Document Basics chapter first, followed by the Quick Tour and each of the five steps.

- **If you're familiar with topic-based authoring tools**, scan the Document Basics chapter to learn basic Flare terminology. Then begin with the Quick Tour, followed by each of the five steps.

> **Note** — Depending on whether you're creating online or print output, you will use *either* Step 5A: Create Print Output *or* Step 5B: Create Online Output. However, if you want to produce *both* types of output from a single project, you will use both of these steps.

GOT FEEDBACK?

We love to hear from our readers!

Your comments and suggestions are welcome. Please contact us at:

info@NorthCoastWriters.com

Document Basics

In this chapter …
- About topic-based authoring
- Terms to understand
- About print documents
- About online documents
- What's next?

OVERVIEW

This chapter provides an overview of topic-based authoring and how Flare is used to create documents that are topic-based. It also describes terminology and capabilities that will familiarize you with some of the language and concepts used in the remainder of this book.

WHAT IS TOPIC-BASED AUTHORING?

According to a recent Wikipedia post, topic-based authoring is:

… a modular content creation approach (popular in the technical publications and documentation arenas) that supports XML content reuse, content management, and makes the dynamic assembly of personalized information possible.

Say what? Let's clarify that.

- **Modular content creation** — As simple as it sounds, the heart of topic-based authoring is creating topics. Modular simply means that content exists in units—called topics.

- **XML content reuse, content management** — Topics are discrete units of information, which makes them easy to reuse and maintain.

- **Dynamic assembly of personalized information** — Because topics are discrete units of information, they can be combined in various ways for customized results.

HOW TRADITIONAL AND TOPIC-BASED DOCUMENTS DIFFER

When you write a *traditional*, print-based document, you organize information—**content**—in a linear fashion, usually to be read front to back. With larger documents, you use various **navigational aids** to help readers find information quickly, such as a Table of Contents, index, and cross-references.

When you write a *topic-based* document, rather than concern yourself with the order of content, you typically develop content—divided into several **topics**—in a way that you can easily rearrange to produce output tailored to different needs.

With *online topic-based* documents, readers point-and-click to obtain information when they need it instead of reading in a linear fashion. With *print topic-based* documents, readers might still choose to read in a linear fashion, but more likely, they'll read only the topics of interest and they'll find those topics by using navigational tools, such as a Table of Contents, index, and cross-references.

WHAT FLARE DOES FOR YOU

Here's a brief sampling of what Flare lets you decide:

- Which topics to include in a document

- How topics will be assembled and organized

- The navigational tools used to help readers find the topics they need

- How content will be reused in the print and online worlds

- Which content will be included in various topics (Flare lets you exclude content from a topic as well as exclude topics themselves.)

The important thing to take away is that when you create documents with Flare, they will be topic-based, not linear. With Flare projects, you'll be able to reuse content and maintain it much more easily.

TERMS TO UNDERSTAND

Topic-based authoring and Flare itself both have unique terminology that you'll see throughout this book. Take a moment to review this list so you won't be caught off-guard when you see these terms.

- **Output** — What is created after you build a Flare project. This will be either a print document (e.g., Word, FrameMaker, PDF file) or an online document (Help system or knowledge base).

Output consists of one or more files and folders, depending on the type of output you build.

> **Note** — Although a PDF file is delivered online, it is considered a print document.

- **Target** — A Flare file that you create that defines characteristics about the type of output to be built. When you build your output, you select the target to build it from. Your project can have many targets. For example, you might have two WebHelp targets for two different levels of software, such as a regular and light. One target is designated as "primary." (For more information, see "Primary targets" on page 239.)

- **Build** — The process of creating output for the selected target using Flare project files.

- **Distribute** — Giving Flare output to others. The output type determines the files you need to send. You may distribute Flare output to colleagues, users, software developers, or your IT staff for further usage.

- **Publish** — Copying online output to a location such as a website, a network, or a hard drive. Publishing does not create the output; it simply transfers it. However, for new users, we discourage this practice until you're more familiar with Flare.

BUILD, GENERATE, COMPILE: WHAT'S THE DIFFERENCE?

You're likely to see several terms that mean the same thing when you use the Flare Help system. We've tried to remain consistent in this book, but use this formula to help you:

Generate = Compile = **Build** (our term)

Just remember: **build** is the process of creating your **output**, based on the **target** you select.

ABOUT PRINT DOCUMENTS

Flare can be used to create five types of print documents:

- Microsoft Word

- Adobe FrameMaker

- Adobe PDF

- Microsoft XPS

- XHTML

Step 5A: Create Print Output, describes in detail these types of print documents and what you need to do to create them. Step 5A also contains instructions for creating a simple print document and a tutorial for creating a more complex print document that includes a Table of Contents and alternating headers and footers.

ABOUT ONLINE DOCUMENTS

Online documents typically refer to Help systems and knowledge bases. You can create both types of online documents with Flare.

For detailed information about creating online documents after you have finished developing your content, see Step 5B: Create Online Output.

HELP SYSTEMS

A Help system is a method of delivering topic-based information to users from within a software application. When a user clicks the application's Help menu, the Help system opens.

A Help system includes a Table of Contents, an index, and the ability to search for words in help topics. Help systems created with Flare also allow users to rate the usefulness of help topics.

Context-sensitive help

A context-sensitive help system is one in which topic-based information is accessed from buttons placed on dialogs and windows in a software application. In such systems, a software developer places a button on a window or dialog for which a writer has written a help topic. When a user clicks the button, it opens a help topic that provides information about the window or dialog.

Flare includes context-sensitive help on some of its dialogs as shown next.

Figure DB-1:
Help button
in Flare
Help

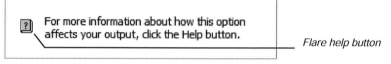

Flare help button

KNOWLEDGE BASES

Knowledge bases are collections of information, often used to share knowledge in an organization or to supplement a Help system. The contents of a knowledge base are documents, such as frequently asked questions, user documentation, and articles.

The primary differences between a knowledge base and a Help system are:

- A knowledge base is not opened from within a software application.

- A knowledge base cannot contain context-sensitive help topics.

Knowledge bases are stored online and are searchable much like Help systems. Users may also browse through topics to find what they need.

ONLINE DOCUMENT FORMATS

Flare can create online documents in any of the following formats:

- DotNet Help

- Microsoft HTML Help

- WebHelp

- WebHelp Plus

- WebHelp AIR

Each of these formats is described in Table 5B-1on page 231.

Choosing the right format

Your work environment may only support certain online document formats. It's a good idea to contact technical personnel in your organization to understand which format they expect you to create.

The following table briefly outlines why you would want to choose certain online document formats. The Flare Help system contains additional information about these formats.

Table DB-1:
Choosing
online
document
formats

Choose this format ...	When ...
DotNet Help	<ul><li>You need to support Microsoft .NET® applications.</li><li>Your HTML Help is inadequate for various reasons.</li><li>You want users to be able to choose to view the output in English, French, German or Japanese (via MadCap Help Viewer).</li><li>You want users to be able to search by using wildcards.</li></ul>
HTML Help	<ul><li>You need to support 32-bit Microsoft Windows® applications.</li><li>Users will be using Internet Explorer®. (Users must use Internet Explorer version 4.0 or later running on Windows 95 or later.)</li><li>Users are not connected to a network.</li><li>You want a single file for your output.</li></ul>
WebHelp	<ul><li>You need to distribute output to the Internet or an Intranet.</li><li>You want to create output in various languages (by using language skins).</li><li>You want to include online documentation in a desktop application.</li><li>Users are using different Internet browsers or platforms.</li></ul>

Table DB-1: (Cont.)	Choose this format ...	When ...

	WebHelp Plus	• You need to support Windows XP or Windows Server® 2003.
		• You want all of the WebHelp features plus:
		  - Quicker user searches
		  - The ability to perform searches for non-XHTML files, such as PDFs or Excel files, that may or may not be part of your project
		  - The ability to merge Flare output so it appears as a single Help system

	WebHelp AIR	• You want all of the WebHelp features plus:
		  - You want a single file for your output.
		  - Your users will store and open your output locally (not from a server or website).
		To create online documents in WebHelp AIR:
		• You and users must install Abobe® AIR™ (go to http://get.adobe.com/air/ for a free download).
		• You must install Java Runtime Environment (go to http://java.sun.com/javase/downloads/index.jsp for a free download).

HOW ONLINE OUTPUT LOOKS (SKINS)

The appearance of online output is controlled by a **skin**. A skin is a file that stores settings that determine how your online output looks (size, position), including its features (Table of Contents, index, glossary, search) and buttons.

Flare comes packaged with a default skin, which is automatically added to each new project you create. The default skin is located in the Skins folder of the Project Organizer.

Figure DB-2:
Skins folder
of the
Project
Organizer

A Flare project can have multiple skins. For example, you might have different skins for different types of online output.

You can change the appearance of online output by editing the skin. See "Editing a skin" on page 237.

WHAT'S NEXT?

Before you tackle your first Flare project, take a look at the next chapter, "A Quick Tour." It will help you become more familiar with the Flare user interface before you begin using the product.

Then proceed to Step 1: Get Started, where you'll start planning and creating your first Flare project.

A Quick Tour

In this chapter ...
- About the images in this book
- What you see when you open Flare
- Left pane
- Middle pane
- Right pane
- Toolbars
- Status bar
- About the Flare workspace

OVERVIEW

Flare is a powerful tool for developing topic-based documents, both online and in print. However, its flexible user interface can be a challenge for new users.

This chapter describes the basic elements of the Flare user interface. In our examples, we'll show you how Flare looks in Windows Vista®, which will give you an idea of what to expect when you start using Flare for yourself. When you become more comfortable using Flare, you'll probably want to adjust the user interface as you prefer.

THE FLARE WORKSPACE

When you first open Flare, you'll see a Getting Started Wizard as shown in Figure QT-1. After you use or close the wizard, you'll see the Flare **workspace** as shown in Figure QT-2. Notice that the Flare workspace contains a left, middle, and right pane, each of which is discussed next.

ABOUT ACTIVE PANES AND WINDOWS

In the Flare workspace, toolbars and menu options will change, depending on which part of the workspace is **active**. This concept applies to tabs in the middle pane as well.

To make a pane or tab active, simply click in the desired part of the workspace. Unavailable options are dimmed.

Figure QT-1:
Getting
Started
Wizard

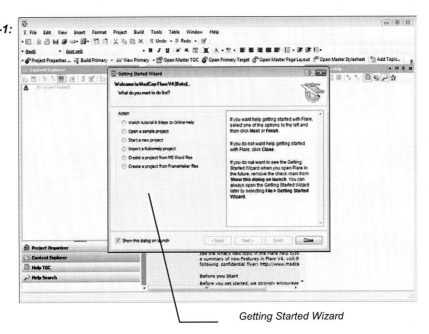

Getting Started Wizard

Figure QT-2:
Flare
workspace

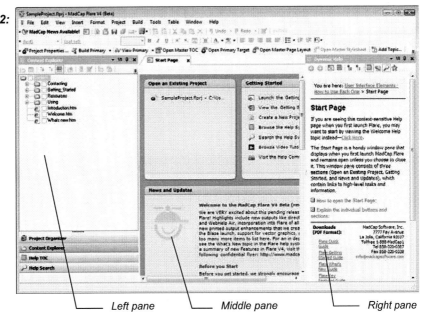

Left pane   Middle pane   Right pane

LEFT PANE

The left pane of the Flare workspace helps you organize and move among the parts of your Flare project.

ACCORDION BARS

In the left pane, you'll notice **accordion bars** as shown in Figure QT-3. Accordion bars indicate which window is active. You can easily switch from one window to another by clicking its accordion bar, which brings the window to the front and makes it active.

Figure QT-3:
Left pane
accordion
bars

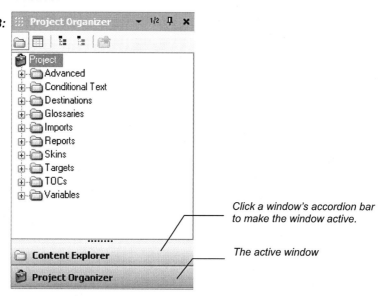

Click a window's accordion bar
to make the window active.

The active window

When you begin using Flare, the **Project Organizer** and **Content Explorer** open in the left pane, both of which you'll use often.

> **Note** — If there isn't enough room to show accordion bars for all of the open windows, you'll see icons directly below the accordion bars as shown in Figure QT-4. Just click an icon to open the window and make it active.

Figure QT-4:
Icon for
additional
windows

Click an icon to view the
window and make it active.

PROJECT ORGANIZER

The Project Organizer is used to view parts of your Flare project and open them in the middle pane. Figure QT-5 shows how the Project Organizer looks when fully expanded.

Click **Expand All** to view all files
in the Project Organizer.

Figure QT-5:
Expanded
Project
Organizer

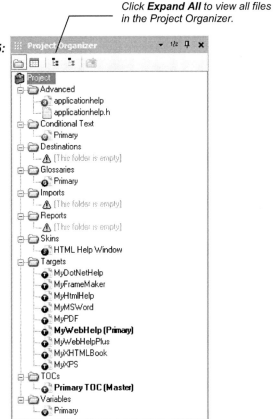

You don't need to understand all of the folders and files in the Project Organizer right now, but you will use them frequently as you create your projects.

> **Note** — Double-clicking a file in the Project Organizer opens it in the middle pane.

CONTENT EXPLORER

You'll use the Content Explorer to open and move among topics in your Flare project. **Topics** can contain text, images, audio files, movie files, and other items.

Figure QT-6 shows how the Content Explorer looks after you create a few topics. Notice that it contains several folders in addition to topic files (HTM) and other types of files.

Click **Expand All** to view all files
in the Content Explorer.

Figure QT-6:
Expanded
Content
Explorer

As shown above, every new Flare project contains a **Resources** folder that holds parts of your project that are not topics, such as images, master pages and page layouts. You'll learn more about these items later.

MIDDLE PANE

When you first launch Flare, the middle pane shows the Start Page (Figure QT-2), a handy place to open a project, view news from MadCap, or submit feature requests and bug reports.

Most of the time, the middle pane shows one of Flare's numerous editors. Figure QT-7 shows the middle pane with four editors open: the XML Editor (active), the TOC Editor (Primary TOC) and two others.

In some editors, it's common to have several items of the same type open. For example, you can have several topics open at the same time, each in their own instance of the XML Editor.

> *Tip* — As you work with Flare, you're bound to lose track of what's open in the middle pane. When this happens, first save all open documents by clicking **Save All** on the Standard toolbar, and then click **Windows → Close All Documents** or **Close All Documents Except This One** (meaning the active document). You can also close a single document by clicking **x** on its tab.

Editor name   *Active editor*   *Editor tabs show file names.*

Figure QT-7:
*Open editors
in the middle
pane*

> *Tip* — To close a file, click **x** on its tab.

In some editors, you may also see tabs along left edge as shown in Figure QT-8. In such instances, the highlighted tab is the open one.

Figure QT-8:
*Tabs along
the left
edge of an
editor*

Tabs ————

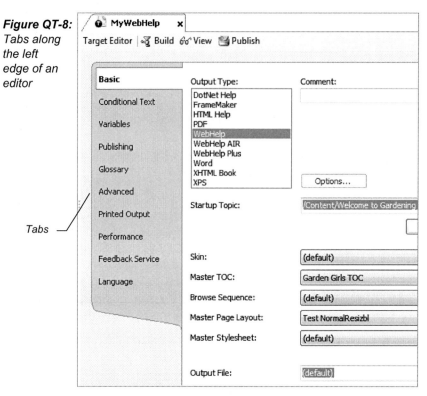

Now let's look at a few commonly used editors.

XML EDITOR

The XML Editor, shown in Figure QT-9, is used to create and edit
topics. You'll use this editor to:

- Enter, edit, and format text

- Insert images, symbols, links, and cross-references

- Create and format tables and lists

Despite this editor's name, you don't need to know anything about
XML in order to use it.

With the XML Editor, you can view content in two modes:

- **Web Layout mode** — To see how a topic would look as online
  output (Help systems and knowledge bases).

- **Print Layout mode** — To see how a topic would look as print output (such as Word or PDF files).

Figure QT-9:
XML Editor

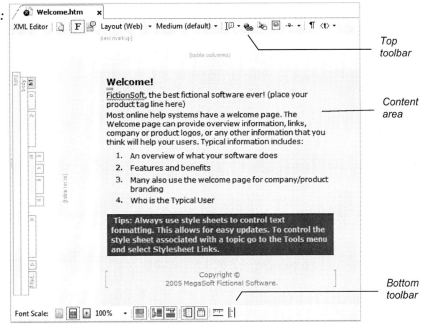

Top toolbar

Content area

Bottom toolbar

Regardless of the mode, the XML Editor has three main parts:

- **Top toolbar** — To switch viewing modes and add things such as links, cross-references and images.

- **Content area** — To enter, edit, and format content.

- **Bottom toolbar** — To magnify text and view XML Editor components, such as rulers and structure bars.

The XML Editor is more fully described in Step 2: Learn the XML Editor, and Appendix C: XML Editor Reference.

TOC EDITOR

The Table of Contents (TOC) Editor is used to create a Table of Contents, which is used to organize and open topics.

Double-clicking a TOC in the Project Organizer opens that TOC in the TOC Editor (Figure QT-11). You can name your TOC files as you please.

Figure QT-10:
*TOC file in
the Project
Organizer*

Double-click a TOC file to
open it in the TOC Editor.

Like other editors, the TOC Editor opens in the middle pane with its own toolbar. Figure QT-11 shows how a fully expanded TOC in the TOC Editor looks.

You'll learn more about using the TOC Editor in Step 4: Create Navigation Aids.

Click **Expand All** to view all files
in the TOC Editor.

Figure QT-11:
Fully
expanded
files in the
TOC Editor

RIGHT PANE

The right pane houses a variety of windows, such as the Spell Check window and Flare's Help system. As in the left pane, each window has an accordion bar, and some also have their own toolbars.

You'll learn more about the contents of the right pane in other chapters.

TOOLBARS

As you've already learned, many editors and windows in Flare have their own toolbars, which apply only to their individual windows.

Flare also has several global toolbars that are always in view (as long as you haven't hidden them), regardless of what else is open. Let's take a quick look.

> *Tip* — Certain options on the global toolbars may be dimmed (unavailable), depending on which window is active.

STANDARD TOOLBAR

The Standard toolbar (Figure QT-12) offers many of the shortcuts seen in other Windows applications, such as opening projects, cutting and pasting, and saving files. It also includes Flare shortcuts, such as **Open the Start Page** and **Source Control**.

Figure QT-12: *Standard toolbar*

PROJECT TOOLBAR

The Project toolbar (Figure QT-13) contains shortcuts for common project tasks, such as building your output (like a Help system or print document). You can also add topics to your project using this toolbar. (To conserve space, we show some of this toolbar's buttons on a pull-down list at the far right.)

> ***Note*** — Drop-down arrows to the right of the Build Primary and View Primary buttons let you select a target other than the primary to build or view.

Figure QT-13: *Project toolbar*

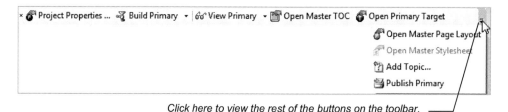

Click here to view the rest of the buttons on the toolbar.

TEXT FORMAT TOOLBAR

The Text Format (Figure QT-14) toolbar offers shortcuts for applying styles and other formatting to text.

Figure QT-14: *Text Format toolbar*

REVIEW TOOLBAR

The Review toolbar includes shortcuts for tasks related to documentation reviews. For example, you'll find shortcuts for emailing a topic to reviewers, inserting and editing annotations (review comments), and importing a reviewed topic.

This book does not cover inserting or processing annotations or conducting documentation reviews.

STATUS BAR

As of Flare Version 4.0, Flare automatically scans your project with its internal analyzer whenever you open it. (A more robust external analyzer—MadCap Analyzer™—can be purchased separately.) You can see the results of the scan in the Status bar at the bottom of the Flare workspace (Figure QT-15).

This book describes how to use the internal analyzer (see Appendix E: Troubleshoot). To learn about the external analyzer, search on "About Analyzer" in the Flare Help system.

Results of the internal analyzer's scan

Figure QT-15:
Status bar

WHAT'S NEXT?

Let's get started!

Move on to Step 1: Get Started, where you'll plan your project and learn about a few common features.

Step 1:
Get Started

In this chapter ...

> Plan your Flare project
> Use our Flare roadmap
> Create a Flare project
> Add a topic
> Preview a topic
> Open a topic
> Check spelling
> Add a target
> Save your work
> Create a topic template

OVERVIEW

We've found that a bit of planning is the key to satisfaction and success with Flare. If you take the time to plan out your project, the learning curve will be shorter and you'll be happier with the outcome—plus you can focus on only the Flare features you need.

To help you get started, we've created a series of planning worksheets in Appendix A: Planning Worksheets, which are intended to be used together. In this chapter, you'll learn what you need to think about, which decisions to make up front, and where to go from here.

PLANNING YOUR FLARE PROJECT

To plan your Flare project, make a copy of Parts 1, 2, and 3 in Appendix A: Planning Worksheets, and answer these questions.

DO YOU HAVE EXISTING SOURCE CONTENT?

If no, then you'll be typing your content directly into Flare.

If yes, then you'll also need to answer these questions using Part 1 of Appendix A:

- What form is your source content in (Word, FrameMaker, HTML, print, other)?

- Do you need to keep the source content and the Flare content in synch when the content changes? Do both need to be updated?

- Will you maintain the content by using the source application (Word, FrameMaker, etc.) or by using Flare? In other words, do you want changes to flow from content in the source application to Flare or do you want to make changes only in Flare?

WHAT KIND OF OUTPUT DO YOU WANT TO CREATE?

You can create output that will be used online or printed. Use Part 2 of Appendix A to complete this information.

Print output can be any of the following:

- Microsoft Word document

- Adobe FrameMaker document

- Adobe PDF file

- Microsoft XPS file (Flare Version 4.0 and later)

- XHTML (Flare Version 4.0 and later)

Online output can be any of the following:

- Microsoft HTML Help

- DotNet Help

- WebHelp

- WebHelp Plus

- WebHelp AIR

See the Document Basics chapter for more information about the types of output you can create with Flare.

HOW WILL CONTENT BE REVIEWED?

How content gets reviewed depends on the software your reviewers have and their preferred way of working. Use Part 3 of Appendix A to identify how content will be reviewed.

With Flare, you can choose to have reviewers:

- **Review topics in Flare or Madcap X-Edit™** (any version—Full, Contribute, or Review). You give reviewers one or more topics from Flare. Reviewers view those topics with Flare or X-Edit and annotate them. You receive annotated topics from reviewers and use Flare to accept or dismiss them. (X-Edit Review is distributed free of charge by MadCap Software.)

  Tip — This scenario is the most efficient. We suggest that you give it a try.

- **Review topics in Word or FrameMaker.** You give reviewers Word or FrameMaker documents with the topics to be reviewed. When you receive comments (in either electronic or printed

form), you incorporate them by typing changes directly into
Flare topics.

- **Review printed documents and write their comments by hand.**
  You give reviewers printed Flare topics or a PDF document with
  the topics to be reviewed. When you receive handwritten
  comments, you incorporate them by typing changes directly into
  Flare topics.

WHAT'S NEXT?

Ready to press on?

Let's take a look at a "roadmap" to help you navigate from here, so
you can ignore the features that don't pertain to your project.

ROADMAP FOR USING FLARE

When you begin using Flare, you may find the user interface and the
huge range of options a bit overwhelming. We created a roadmap to
help you determine the features you need to use for your project.

Again, follow along in Appendix A and complete the worksheets to
get started.

HOW TO USE THIS ROADMAP

Start with "Basic tasks," which you'll need to complete for every
Flare project.

Next, look at "What's your input?" **Input** is your source content. On
the left, find the column that represents the type of input you're
working with. The right column shows the tasks for each input type.

Lastly, look at "What's your output?" **Output** is what you want to
create. On the left, find the column that represents the type of output
you want to create (online or print output). Review the decisions you
need to make and complete the tasks in the right column.

BASIC TASKS

For every Flare project, do these tasks ...

- Create a new Flare *project*—the structure that contains your content and the project's supporting files (page 39).

- (*Initially*) Apply styles from the default Flare stylesheet (Styles.css) to control the appearance of topic content (page 136).

- (*Eventually*) Create your own topic and table stylesheets and the styles they contain. Then apply your own styles to content.

> **Note**— You can easily attach your own stylesheet to a project or to individual topics and apply your own styles later, after you have more experience with Flare.

WHAT'S YOUR INPUT?

Input type	Decide ...	Do these tasks ...
No existing electronic source content	Which topics will you include? Which images will you include?	• Create an outline for the Table of Contents (not a Flare task). It doesn't have to be perfect since you can easily change the Flare TOC at any time. • Create content with Flare's XML Editor. Type text, create lists and tables, insert images, add other optional elements (such as snippets and variables) to topics (Step 2: Learn the XML Editor, Step 3: Develop Content, Step 4: Create Navigation Aids, and Appendix F: Single-Sourcing).

Input type	Decide ...	Do these tasks ...
Word or FrameMaker files	Which application will you use to maintain the content—Flare or the source application?	▪ Prepare your Word or FrameMaker document for importing (page 260). ▪ Set up the import details (how to handle styles, where to split content into topics, whether to link source files to Flare, whether to use Easy Sync for automatic importing of changed source files, etc.; page 260). ▪ Import the content (pages 267 for Word and 276 for FrameMaker).
HTML files	Do you want to keep source content styles or use a Flare stylesheet?	▪ Import the content (page 286).
X-Edit (Full or Contribute)		▪ Receive topics via email from an X-Edit author. ▪ Incorporate topics into your project. *Note*— You can also receive stylesheets and page layout files from X-Edit Full or Contribute.

WHAT'S YOUR OUTPUT?

Output type	Decide …	Do these tasks …
Online output	Which topics will you include? How will you structure topics in the TOC? Which images will you include? How will your final output look (fonts, colors, spacing)? Will you use the default skin or a custom skin? (Custom skins are not covered in this book.)	▪ Create online navigation aids (TOC, index entries, links). See Step 4: Create Navigation Aids, on page 143. ▪ (*If you want headers, footers, or mini-tocs*) Create a master page and set up headers and footers. See procedure beginning on page 236. ▪ (*If you want to change the appearance of the skin*) Edit the default skin (or one of your own). See page 237 ▪ Set up the target with the output file name, TOC name, condition tags to include or exclude, and master page (if using one). See page 216. ▪ Build the online output. See Step 5B: Create Online Output, on page 242. ▪ Test the online output. See page 243. ▪ Deliver the online output. All of these are described in Step 4: Create Navigation Aids, and Step 5B: Create Online Output.

Output type	Decide …	Do these tasks …
Print output	Which type of print output do you want to create? (PDF, Word, FrameMaker, XPS*, XHTML*)	■ Add optional elements (images, cross-references, snippets, variables).
	What will the print output contain (Table of Contents, index, glossary)?	■ (Depending on your decisions) Create topics for front and back matter elements, such as a print TOC and print index. See page 193.
	Do you need a simple layout or a more complex layout with different headers, footers, or page-number formats for front matter, chapters, and back matter?	■ Create a topic outline (a Flare TOC) that indicates the topics to be included in the print output. See page 197.
	How should the output be laid out (headers, footers, page numbers)?	■ (Depending on your decisions) Set up and customize page layouts (headers and footers). See procedure beginning on page 201.
		■ (If you set up page layouts) Set chapter breaks by linking page layouts to topics in the topic outline (Flare TOC). See procedure beginning on page 213
		■ Set up the target with the output file name, outline TOC name, page layout names, and condition tags to include or exclude. See page 216.
		■ Build the print output. See page 217.
		All of these are described in the chapters for Step 3: Develop Content, Step 4: Create Navigation Aids, and Step 5A: Create Print Output.

* Flare Version 4.0 and later.

Common tasks

There are certain tasks that you'll do over and over again in Flare, so we've grouped them here. They consist of:

- Creating a Flare project

- Adding a topic

- Previewing a topic

- Checking spelling

- Adding a target

- Saving your work

Always consult the roadmap beginning on page 35 if you're uncertain where to begin.

CREATING A FLARE PROJECT

Regardless of what you're creating and where the content comes from, you always need to create a Flare **project** to hold your content. Let's get to it!

A project is like a container that holds related information (topics, TOCs, image files, dictionary, stylesheet) in a single unit.

Flare simplifies the process of creating a project by providing a wizard, which walks you through the choices you need to make. The wizard creates the project framework, to which you'll add topics, and possibly a TOC and index.

Before using the Start New Project Wizard next, use Part 4 of Appendix A to decide:

- Where you will store your project if not in the default folder

- If a source control application will be used (optional)

Using the Start New Project Wizard

Use this procedure to create a new project.

When you launch Flare, the Getting Started Wizard opens first, as you read about in the Quick Tour chapter. If you select **Start a new project**, Flare opens the Start New Project Wizard.

The **Start New Project Wizard** asks you to make choices about your project. Just click **Next** to move from one screen to the next. As you move through the screens, you can accept the default settings for all remaining choices by clicking **Finish** instead of **Next**. This closes the wizard and skips additional choices.

> ***An exception*** — If you create the project and import the content simultaneously, you don't have to use the wizard. However, for simplicity, we don't cover that feature in this guide. To learn more about this option, open the Flare Help system and search on "Creating a project by importing."

To keep things simple, we'll take you through the steps for creating a new project that is *not* bound to a source control application. If you want your Flare project to be bound to a source control application (such as Microsoft Visual Source Safe®), see "Binding your project to a source control application" on page 42.

To create a project:

1. Select **File → New Project**. The Start New Project Wizard opens.

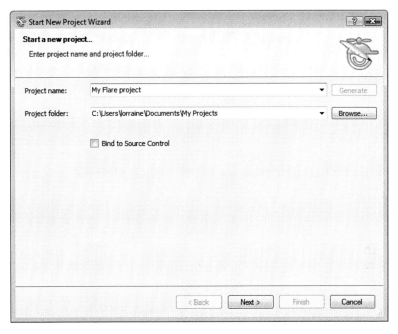

2. Type a unique project name.

3. (*Optional*) To save your project in a folder other than the default, click **Browse** and select a different folder.

4. (*Optional*) To use a source control application with your Flare project, see "Binding your project to a source control application," next.

5. Select the language you want Flare to use when spell-checking your topics.

6. Select **Factory Templates** from the Template Folders section, and **Empty** from the Templates section.

> *Note* — As you gain experience, you'll probably want to use one of your own templates ("My Templates") for new projects instead of using factory templates. To learn how to create a template, see "Creating a topic template" on page 60.
>
> Also, selecting "Application Help Sample" gives you a TOC with links to starter topics. This is an alternative to starting from scratch.

7.   From the list of Available Targets, select the type of output you want to create.

8.   Click **Create the project,** then click **Finish**.

The Content Explorer (left pane) lists your first topic, "Topic.htm" and a Resources folder for project resources (such as images).

> **Best Practice** — Store a backup copy of your entire project on a server or secondary storage device, and back up often!

Binding your project to a source control application

Binding your project to a source control application is optional. Source control applications can help you to manage your Flare content by allowing you to coordinate and control changes to it. This is especially helpful when:

- Multiple authors need access to content.

- Authors need to store backup versions of files as they change.

Binding (linking) your Flare project to a source control application lets you take advantage of your source control application's version control and change control features.

When you create a Flare project, you can indicate which source control application you are using and where to store Flare project files within it. The source control application manages versions of project files as they change and prevents multiple users from accessing the same file simultaneously.

Flare provides *programmatic support* for Microsoft Visual Source Safe (VSS) and Microsoft Team Foundation Server (TFS). This means that tasks such as checking in and checking out files, and adding files to source control *can* be done from within Flare.

Because Flare files are stored in XML format, Flare is *compatible* with all source control applications on the market. This means that you can add your project files to any source control application to use that application's source control features. However, for applications other than VSS and TFS, source control tasks, such as checking in or checking out files, *cannot* be done automatically from within Flare.

> ***Note*** — To use a source control application other than VSS and TFS directly from Flare, see "Using an API to Integrate Source Control" in the Flare Help system. You can also search on "source control" in the Flare Help system for detailed information about using Flare with a source control application.

The source control application must already be installed on your computer before you can bind a new project to it.

⚙ To create a project that is integrated with source control:

1. Complete Steps 1 – 3 of the procedure for creating a new project (page 40).

2. Click **Bind to Source Control**, then **Next**.

3. Click **Bind Project**, then **Next**.

4. Complete the fields *in one section* of this dialog:

    If you have Visual Source Safe (VSS),

    a. Select **Visual Source Safe**.

    b. Click **Browse** to select the INI file for the VSS database.

    c. Click **Browse** to select the VSS database folder in which to store your Flare project files. (You might need to log on to Visual Source Safe to do this.)

    If you have Team Foundation Server (TSS),

    a. Select **Team Foundation Server**.

    b. In the Server field, type the URL for the server.

    c. Click **Browse** to select the Team Foundation project to bind your Flare project to. (You might need to enter a user name and password to log in to the Team Foundation Server.)

    If you are using a different source control application,

    a. Select **Source Code Control Plug-in**.

b. Select your source control program from the Provider list.

c. Click **Browse** to select the project to bind your Flare project to. (You might need to enter a user name and password to log in.)

5. Click **OK** twice after making your selections.

6. Continue with Step 5 of the procedure for creating a new project. (page 40).

ADDING A TOPIC

Throughout this book, you'll see the words **content** and **topic** used often. Let's take a moment to review what these terms mean:

- A **topic** is the "box" in which content is stored. Each topic is a file (with an .htm extension) that conforms to the XML specification.

- **Content** is various types of information contained in a topic, such as text, tables, lists, and images.

- A **project** is simply a collection of topics and related files, which are stored in project folders.

To create a new project, you'll create Flare topics and add content to them. Your content can be new or imported (see Appendix B: Import Content, for more about importing content).

Methods used to add a topic

You can add topics from the TOC, from the Content Explorer, or by using the Project menu. Which method should you use? Read on ...

Table 1-1:
Methods used to add a topic

To ...	Do this ...
Create a topic *and* add it to a TOC (and save time)	Add a topic from the TOC. This method adds a topic to your project and to your TOC simultaneously—plus it automatically links the topic to the TOC entry it creates. (A TOC entry must link to a topic in order to open that topic in the output.)

Table 1-1: *(Cont.)*	To ...	Do this ...
	Quickly add a topic when you don't need a TOC	Add a topic using the Content Explorer or Project menu.
		This method adds a topic without linking it to a TOC entry. This option is a good choice when you're creating websites and short documents that don't need a TOC.

> *Note* — If you decide to add a TOC later, you can do so easily. See "Creating a Table of Contents" on page 144.

To add a topic:

1. Make sure that the Flare project to which you want to add topics is open.

2. If you need a TOC, take these steps. Otherwise, skip to Step 3, next.

   a. Select the Project Organizer.

   b. Expand the TOCs folder.

   c. Double-click the TOC you want to open. The TOC Editor opens in the middle pane.

   d. On the TOC Editor's toolbar, click **Create a new topic and link to it** .

   e. Skip to Step 4 below.

3. If you don't need a TOC, do one of the following:

   - Select **Project → Add Topic**.

     or

   - On the Content Explorer toolbar, click **Create a new Topic file** .

4. Fill in the fields on the Add New Topic dialog.

Option	Description
Template Folders	Folders that contain templates used to create topics. You can select: • (Recommended) **Factory Templates** to choose a template provided with Flare, or • **My Templates** to choose one of your own topic templates. To learn more about creating your own topic templates, see "Creating a topic template" on page 60.
Templates	A list of the templates in the selected template folder.
Preview	A preview of the selected template.
Source File	The path to the selected template. To use a template that is not stored in the My Templates folder, click [...] and browse for the desired HTM file. The file must be in XML format (such as a topic file from the open project or another Flare project).

Option	Description
Folder	(*Optional*) The sub-folders contained in the Content Explorer's Content folder. Select the sub-folder to store the topic in.
File name	The file name for the topic.
	Best Practice — For ease of maintenance, the File name and topic title should match.
1st Heading	The topic title. Leave this field blank if you want the topic title to match your topic file name (recommended).
Style	The style for the 1st Heading (topic title). Leave this field blank if you want the topic title to use Flare's h1 style (recommended for new users).
Stylesheet	Flare automatically attaches the default stylesheet to the topic.

5. Click **Add**, then **OK** to copy the new topic to your project.

The new topic opens in the XML Editor and is added to the list of topics in the Content Explorer. If you added the topic from a TOC, the new topic is also added to the TOC.

New topic in Content Explorer

New topic in XML Editor

Now you can add content to your topic in the form of text, lists, tables, audio files, movies, and images.

PREVIEWING A TOPIC

Previewing a topic lets you:

- See what the topic will look like when it is built.

- Test the topic's links before you build the output.

You can preview the topic that is active in the XML Editor. When you preview the topic, you can include or exclude text that is tagged with a condition tag.

The primary target's type determines the format Flare uses for the preview.

Table 1-2:
Formats used to show topic previews

If the primary target type is ...	Flare uses this format for preview ...
Online	DotNet Help
PDF	Adobe PDF
XPS	Microsoft XPS
XHTML	Print Layout mode
Word or FrameMaker	*Preview is not available for these targets.*

> *Note* — To designate a target as primary, right-click the target in the Project Organizer and select **Make Primary** from the menu.

To preview a topic:

1. Click **Preview compiled topic** on the XML Editor's toolbar.

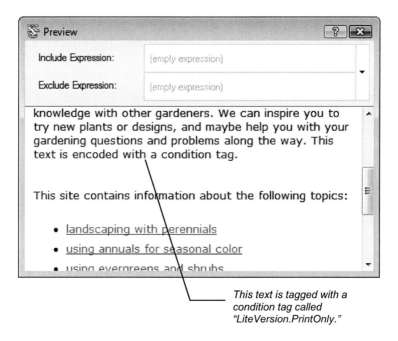

This text is tagged with a condition tag called "LiteVersion.PrintOnly."

2. If you want to include or exclude text that has been tagged with condition tags, click the arrow to the right of the Include and Exclude Expression fields. A list of condition tags opens.

Note — By default all text is included, even if tagged with a condition tag.

3. Check the **Include** or **Exclude** boxes next to the styles to be
    included or excluded, then click **OK**. The tags you checked are
    shown on the Preview window and the applicable text is shown
    or not shown.

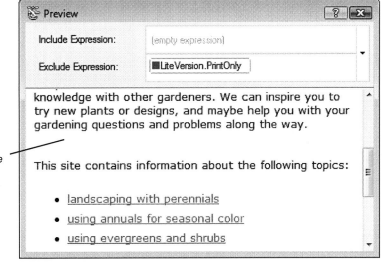

The tagged text is not shown in the Preview window because it was excluded.

4. Close the Preview window by clicking its close button ().

OPENING A TOPIC

You can have several topics open at once, each in its own XML Editor page. Each topic has a tab. The **white tab** indicates which topic is active and visible in the XML Editor window.

Figure 1-1:
An active
topic in the
XML Editor
window

Active topic

To open a topic:

1. Make sure that the Flare project is open and that the Content Explorer is in view.

2. Do one of the following:

    - Double-click the topic in the Content Explorer. (If you've created sub-folders in the Content Explorer, you might have to expand a sub-folder to find the topic.)

    - If the project's TOC is open and in view in the middle pane, right-click the topic in the TOC and select **Open Link** from the menu.

    > **Note** — You can also open a topic from the TOC, if the **Toggle the double-click behavior: open topic or run properties dialog** button on the XML Editor toolbar is set to open topics, not topic properties. We recommend that you leave it set this way.

The topic opens in its own XML Editor page in the middle pane.

CHECKING SPELLING

You have these options for spell-checking your project's topics:

- Flare can check spelling as you type, or

- You can check spelling manually.

Checking spelling as you type

Flare can check spelling as you type in the topic (or snippet) currently in view. With this option turned on, Flare highlights possible spelling errors with a red zigzag underline.

Figure 1-2:
A spelling
error

new plants or designs, and maybe
ions and probems along the way.

You can turn this option on or off for individual topics. You might have two topics open and have Spell Check While Typing turned on for one topic and off for the other. If your spelling errors aren't being highlighted in the active topic, you probably have this option turned off for that topic.

To turn on spell-checking while typing:

- Select **Tools → Spell Check While Typing**.

To resolve a potential spelling error:

1. Right-click the word that Flare highlighted. A menu appears listing possible spellings of the word.

flourish.   ~~We hope that we can inspire you~~ to t

design! | problems | arde

probem | probes

                                 | proems

This si1 | problem | llov

• l〔 | poems

• u〔 | probe

• u〔 | proem

• g〔 | robes |

• p〔 | Ignore All | ;ts

• m〔 | Add To Dictionary |

2.   Do one of the following:

To ...	Do this ...
Replace the misspelled word with a suggested word	Select the correct word from the list.
Keep the highlighted word spelled as it is and ignore other instances of this word in this topic file	Select **Ignore All**. This option does not affect other topics. Flare will still flag this word as a possible spelling error in other topics if spell-checking is turned on for those topics.
Keep the highlighted word spelled as it is and add the highlighted word to the dictionary	Select **Add To Dictionary**. If you add the word to the dictionary, Flare will not flag this spelling as questionable in other topics or snippets.

Checking spelling manually

You can have the spell-checker check one or more topics for possible spelling errors in:

▪   The active topic (the one that is currently visible)

▪   All open topics

- All topics in the same folder as the active topic

- All topics (even if not open) in the project

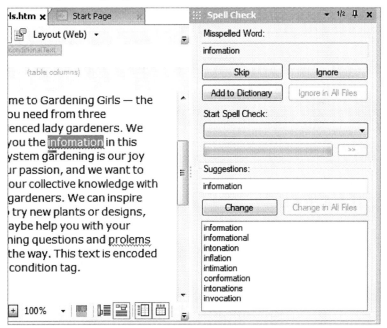 To check spelling in one or more topics:

1. Select **Tools → Spell Check Window**. The Spell Check window opens in the right pane, and the first misspelled word in the active topic is highlighted.

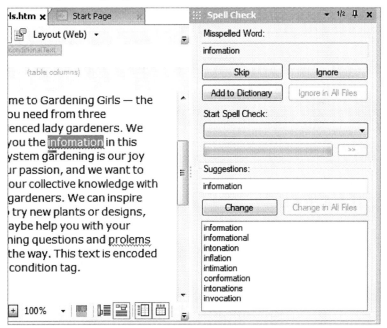

2. To check spelling in the active topic only (the default), skip to Step 4, below.

3. To check spelling in more than one topic, select these options from the Start Spell Check field:

To check spelling in ...	Do this ...
All topics in the open project	Select **whole project**. Flare opens topics that have questionable spellings one at a time in the order in which they are listed in the Content Explorer.

To check spelling in ...	Do this ...
All open topics	Select **all open documents**.
All topics in the same folder as the active topic	Select **documents in same folder**. Flare opens topics with questionable spellings one at a time in the same order in which they are listed in the folder.

4. Do one of the following:

To ...	Do this ...
Change the spelling to a suggested word	Select a suggested word and select **Change**.
Keep the word as it is and move to the next misspelled word	Select **Skip**.
Keep the word as it is, move to the next misspelled word, and ignore other occurrences of this word in this *topic*	Select **Ignore**.
Keep the word as it is, move to the next misspelled word, and ignore all other occurrences of this word in this *project*	Select **Ignore in All Files**.
Keep the word as it is, add the word to the dictionary, and move to the next misspelled word	Select **Add to Dictionary**.

5. When the spell-check is complete, click **OK**.

6. (*Optional*) Close the Spell Check window by clicking its close button (**x**).

7. Click **Save All** to save all spelling corrections and terms you added to the dictionary.

8. (*Optional*) Close the topics that Flare opened due to questionable spellings.

Adding terms to the dictionary

Use this procedure to add new terms to an existing dictionary. (If the dictionary doesn't exist, you can create it by adding a word to it when you check spelling.)

To add terms to a dictionary:

1. If the dictionary already exists in the Project Organizer, expand the **Advanced** folder, then double-click the dictionary. The Dictionary Editor opens in the middle pane, showing current entries.

2. Click **New item** in the Dictionary Editor's toolbar. A new blank line appears.

3. Type the term to be added in the Word column. You can also type a Comment if desired.

4. Click **Save** to save the dictionary file.

ADDING A TARGET

Use the following procedure to add a target to your project.

To add a target to your project:

1. In the Project Organizer, right-click **Targets** and select **Add Target** from the menu. The Add Target dialog opens.

2. In the File Name field, type a name for the new target.

3. Click **Add**, then **OK** to add the new target.

    The new target is listed in the Targets folder and opens in the Target Editor.

4. Set up the target for the type of output you want to create.

    ▪ **To set up a target for print output**, see "Task 8: Set up the print target" on page 216.

    ▪ **To set up a target for online output**, see "Setting up an online target" on page 238.

SAVING YOUR WORK

It's a good idea to save your work periodically instead of waiting until you're ready to exit Flare. There are two ways to save your work:

▪ **Save only the item currently in view.** You might be viewing a topic, a TOC, a list of styles in a stylesheet, a variable list, a list of condition tags, or any other content related to your project.

▪ **Save your entire project.**

As shown in Figure 1-3, Flare lets you know if you have any unsaved work by placing an asterisk (*) to the right of the file name on the tab for any item (topic, TOC, index, stylesheet, import file, etc.) that has changed.

Figure 1-3:
An unsaved
topic

> **Note** — The active topic is the one currently visible in the middle pane of the XML Editor.

As shown in Figure 1-4, there are no unsaved changes in the active topic ("Selecting a tree"), but there are unsaved changes in another open topic ("landscaping with perennials").

Active topic

Figure 1-4:
Unsaved
changes in
an inactive
topic

> **Best Practice** — Use **Save All** routinely to save the changes in all open topics.

To save the active file:

Do one of the following:

- Click **Save File** .
- Select **File → Save**.
- Type **CTRL + S**.

Flare saves the active file (the file shown in the middle pane).

To save your entire project:

Do one of the following:

- Click **Save All** .

- Select **File → Save All**.

- Type **CTRL + SHIFT + S**.

Flare saves all project files.

> *Tip* — As you work with Flare, you're bound to lose track of what's open in the middle pane. When this happens, first save all the open documents, and then click **Windows → Close All Documents** or **Close All Documents Except This One** (meaning the active document). You can also close a single document by clicking **x** on its tab.

CREATING A TOPIC TEMPLATE

You can save a lot of time by creating a topic template for your project. Templates allow you create topics that are consistent in appearance without creating and reformatting elements you use frequently each time you create a new topic.

When you add a new topic using one of your own topic templates, you'll replace any placeholder text with the topic content just as you would do in any template.

> *Note* — A topic template is simply a topic that you move to the My Templates\Content folder, which you create to hold all of your topic templates.

Our recommendations

- Create more than one template to use with different types of topics. For example, you might have one template for overviews, another for step-by-step procedures, and a third for frequently asked questions.

- When you create a template, attach a stylesheet to it and apply styles to text.

- Include an empty formatted table in your template. (You can delete it from topics later if you don't need it.) See "Adding a table" on page 116 for details.

To create a topic template for your project:

1. Open a Flare project and add a new topic *without* adding it to the TOC (see "Adding a topic" on page 45).

2. In the Add New Topic dialog:

   a. Give the topic a meaningful file name (for example, "Concepts.htm" if you're creating a template for concepts).

   b. Click **Add**, then **OK** to create the topic and copy it to your project.

3. Add elements you'll use often, such as paragraphs, headings, tables, and lists.

4. Add any boilerplate text required (see Step 2: Learn the XML Editor).

5. Format each element as you want future topics to look.

6. Save the topic (see "Saving your work" on page 58).

7. In Windows Explorer, find the topic file you just created and copy it (**CTRL + C**). Your topics are listed in the Content folder or a sub-folder of it, depending on how your Content Explorer folders are set up.

Here's an example of a Concepts topic we created for illustration.

8. In Windows Explorer:

    a. Create a folder called **My Templates** in your Documents folder (My Documents on XP systems).

    b. Create a folder called **Content** in the My Templates folder.

9. Press **CTRL + V** to paste the topic file (Concepts.htm in our example) to the My Templates\Content folder you just created.

10. Delete the original topic you created in Step 2 of this procedure. (From Flare's Content Explorer, right-click the topic and select **Delete**.)

    The next time you add a topic, you'll be able to select the topic template from the My Templates folder.

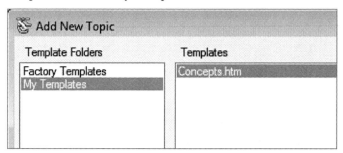

WHAT'S NEXT?

If you've created a project, added a topic to it, and you're not sure what to do next:

- Look at the roadmap beginning on page 35.

- Find the rows that match your scenario.

- Follow the list of tasks in each part of the roadmap.

You might even place a bookmark (the old-fashioned kind) at page 35, because you'll want to come back to the roadmap as you work through your first Flare project. Good luck to you, and enjoy!

OUR RECOMMENDATION

At this point, we strongly recommend that you complete the next chapter, Step 2: Learn the XML Editor. It will give you a solid background in using the XML Editor to add text to a topic as you try out additional features in the remainder of this book.

Step 2:
Learn the
XML Editor

STEP 5: Create Output
5A: Print Output
5B: Online Output

STEP 4:
Create
Nav Aids

STEP 3:
Develop
Content

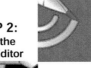

STEP 2:
Learn the
XML Editor

STEP 1:
Get Started

In this chapter ...
- ➤ De-clutter your workspace
- ➤ Enter text
- ➤ View tags
- ➤ View cursors and text blocks
- ➤ Manipulate text
- ➤ Format text
- ➤ View layout modes
- ➤ Create a new topic
- ➤ Save a project

OVERVIEW

This chapter contains a tutorial and supplemental information about using the Flare XML Editor. With the tutorial, you'll learn how to:

- Add topics and enter text into them

- Reveal the tags associated with text

- Change the appearance of text by applying styles and local formatting

- Save your work

You'll also learn about certain elements in the XML Editor that you'll see commonly, such as tags, structure bars, and various types of cursors.

WHAT IS XML?

XML (Extensible Markup Language) is a World Wide Web Consortium (W3C) specification that defines markup languages used to support document sharing.

Content is marked with **tags** that describe the content according to XML rules. In essence, this lets you separate the content from its formatting, making content easy to reuse in other applications or on different computers.

You can even edit XML files in a different XML editor without losing data or formatting. Hence, you are not locked into using the Flare XML Editor if you prefer to use a different one.

TUTORIAL SETUP

Before you begin this tutorial, make sure you have completed these tasks in Step 1: Get Started, using the default values that appear:

- Create a project (page 39)

- Add your first topic (page 45)

Be sure to **set aside 45 minutes** to complete this tutorial chapter. It's better to complete all of the tasks in succession.

TASK 1: DE-CLUTTERING YOUR WORKSPACE

As you learned in Step 1: Get Started, when you create or open a topic, the XML Editor opens in the middle pane. To make viewing cleaner, we recommend de-cluttering your workspace by closing a couple elements you won't be using routinely.

Start page tab

Dynamic Help window

1. Click the **x** in the upper right corner of the Dynamic Help window to close it.

2. Click the red **x** on the Start Page tab to close it. (This maximizes workspace in the XML Editor.)

The XML Editor should now look like this:

TASK 2: ENTERING TEXT

To get started, you'll type a heading and few paragraphs of text, which you'll use to learn more about the XML Editor in the rest of this chapter.

1. Highlight **New Topic** in the XML Editor and type **Welcome**.

    Notice that what you typed replaces the existing placeholder text. You'll also see that the cursor changes shape and a small yellow box appears under the "W," both of which you'll learn more about later.

IntelliSense popup

As you type, you'll probably see the IntelliSense popup as shown above. **IntelliSense** anticipates what you're typing and offers suggestions for automatically completing a word.

If you just keep typing, the IntelliSense popup will disappear. But while learning the XML Editor, we recommend that you disable it. If you want to turn it back on later, see "Disabling and enabling IntelliSense" on page 302.

2. To disable IntelliSense, click **Disable IntelliSense** on the IntelliSense popup the next time it appears. Then click **Yes** on the confirmation box.

3. Highlight **Delete this text and replace it with your own content** and type:

    Welcome to Gardening Girls, the help you need from three experienced lady gardeners. We created this website because gardening is our joy and passion, and we want to share our knowledge with other gardeners.

    As you can see, entering text in the XML Editor is very much like using a word processor, but there are important differences, as you'll learn in a bit. Let's type more text.

4. Press **ENTER** to begin a new paragraph, just as you would with a word processor. Don't worry about the spacing between paragraphs. You'll fix that later.

5. Now enter the following paragraphs:

What we offer

This site contains information about the following topics:

Landscaping with perennials

Using annuals for seasonal color

Growing beautiful gardens in the shade

When you're finished, the XML Editor should look like this:

Tag bars

That's enough typing for now. Let's see how you can view the structure of the text.

TASK 3: VIEWING TAGS

Notice the **tag bars** at the left of your content. Tag bars are a type of structure bar that tells you important information about how your document is constructed. They can also be used to reveal additional options.

Although you can use Flare without knowing anything about XML, we don't want you to be thrown off guard when you see things like "p," "ol," and "li" in the tag bars.

1. Click the **body** tag bar. (Tag bars are highlighted when you place your cursor over them.)

2. From the list, select **Reveal Tags**.

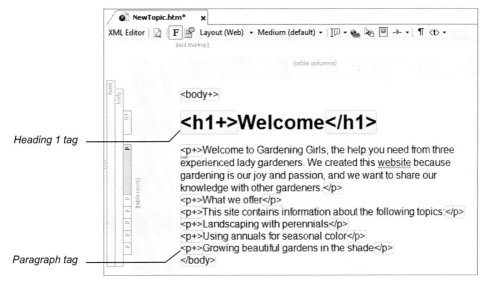

Heading 1 tag —————————

Paragraph tag —————————

Whoa! What just happened? Flare now shows you the **tags** it automatically assigned to the text you entered ("body," "h1" and "p"). These tags were based on the default stylesheet for the "Empty" template you chose in Step 1: Get Started.

Flare also decided where your tags should begin and end, based on when you pressed **ENTER**. The beginning of a tag is followed by a plus sign (as in <h1+> and <p+>) and the end is preceded by a slash (as in </h1> and </p>).

Starting tag ———————   ⌐ *Ending tag*

<p+>Using annuals for seasonal color</p>

So why does this matter? Because the more you use styles to define how your Flare documents will look, the easier it will be to maintain your documents. That goes for tables and images as well as text.

Styles are very complex for new Flare users, and we only touch on them lightly in this book. However, keep in mind that using styles will save you oodles of time maintaining your documents in the future.

Now let's hide the tags to make for easier viewing.

3. Click the **body** structure bar.

4. From the list, select **Reveal Tags**. (This option toggles the tag view on and off.)

Tip — You can also click **Toggle show tags** 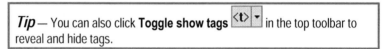 in the top toolbar to reveal and hide tags.

Although tags sound complicated if you're not familiar with them, the good news is that Flare manages XML rules for you so you can't create an XML document that is not well-formed.

With more complex topics, the tag bars will show several additional tags. Here are some of the more common Flare tags.

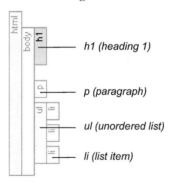

h1 (heading 1)

p (paragraph)

ul (unordered list)

li (list item)

TASK 4: VIEWING CURSORS AND TEXT BLOCKS

Most people use the word **paragraph** to describe a unit of text in a document. Flare uses the term **block** to describe any major unit of content that is within a starting and ending tag.

This is done to avoid confusing the concept of paragraphs with paragraph tags (<p>). In this book, when we talk about units of text, we use the term **text block**.

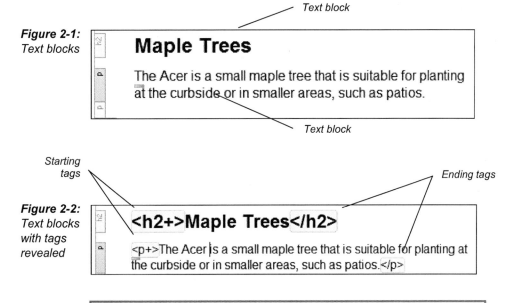

Figure 2-1:
Text blocks

Figure 2-2:
Text blocks with tags revealed

> *Note* — When using the XML Editor, you cannot type more than one consecutive space unless they are non-breaking spaces.

Flare also gives you clues about how tags are attached to your content by changing the shape of the cursor. Let's see how this works.

1. Click after the word "Welcome." Notice how the cursor changes to a right bracket (]).

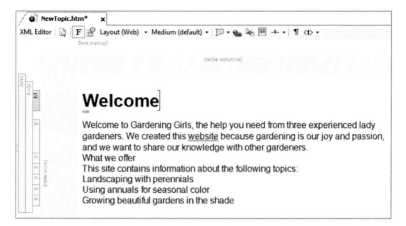

A right bracket indicates that whatever you type will have the characteristics of the text block to the left of the cursor. The tag bar is also highlighted (in this case, h1).

2.   Type **Gardeners!** See how the text takes on the characteristics of the first text block?

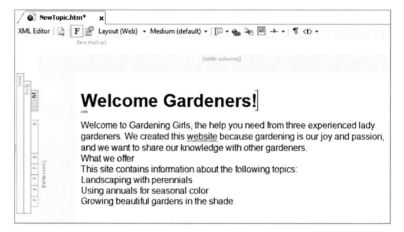

3.   Now click before the "W" in "What we offer." The cursor changes to a left bracket ([), indicating that what you type will have the same formatting as the text block to the right. Notice that the tag bar now shows p as the current tag.

Tag bar

4. Click anywhere in the first paragraph to see how the cursor changes again.

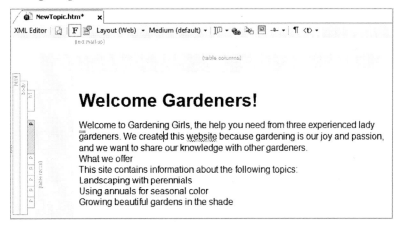

This is the traditional "insert" cursor you're probably used to from word processing.

There are lots of cursors in Flare as described in "Cursor types" on page 294. For now, just make sure you understand how the bracketed cursors work.

TASK 5: MANIPULATING TEXT

The XML Editor works very much like a word processor when it comes to manipulating text.

1. Move your cursor to a new location and click it once, then again and again until you've clicked it a few times in succession. See how Flare progressively selects more and more text as you continue to click?

This is a great shortcut when you want to select words and text blocks for editing. Try it out a few times, and notice how the tag bars change to indicate what is highlighted.

Common editing functions, such as copying and pasting text with shortcut keys, are so much like word processors that you won't try them out here. A complete list of these functions, plus navigation commands such as **PAGE UP** and **HOME**, are listed in "Shortcuts when working with text" on page 297 and "Navigational shortcuts" on page 299 for your reference.

One function that differs is deleting text, because as you'll see, sometimes you want to delete an entire text block *plus* the tags associated with it. Let's try this now.

2. First, click in the word **shade**.

3. Now hover your cursor over the block's tag bar (p). When the cursor changes to a hand 🖑, click the tag bar, then choose **Edit** → **Delete** from the list.

   The entire text block is deleted, including the starting and ending tags.

   You can copy (**CTRL + C**) and paste (**CTRL + V**) text in Flare just as you would in most word processors. (You can copy and paste within a topic, from one topic to another, or from an external source—such as a Microsoft Word document.) In addition, Flare gives you another way to copy and paste. You can use a Flare feature called a tag hint bar to open a context menu that contains copy and paste options. Let's see how this works.

   > **Note** — For more information about tag hint bars, see "Using tag hint bars and context menus" on page 93.

4. First, double-click to select the word **perennials**. Notice the **red tag hint bar** beneath the selected word.

   Red tag hint bar

5. Hover your cursor over the red tag hint bar to expand it. The bar changes to a flashing red rectangle.

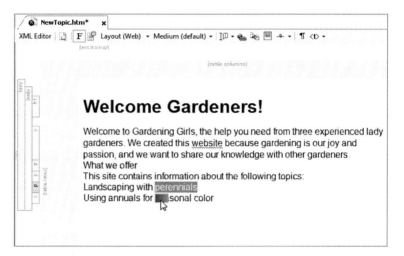

6. Now click the red rectangle to open a drop-down **context menu**.

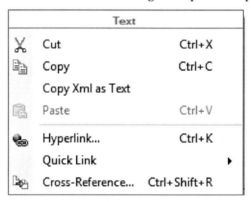

7. Select **Copy**.

8. Click after the word **annuals** and press the **SPACEBAR**.

9. Press **CTRL + V** to paste in the text.

10. Correct the wording by typing a space after perennials and by typing the word **and** between annuals and perennials.

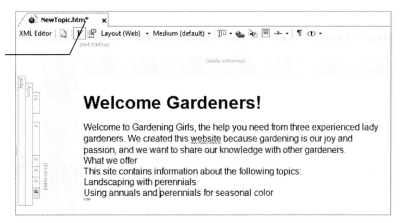

Asterisk indicates unsaved changes in this topic

You can also use yellow tag hint bars and context menus to select options for entire text blocks. For more information about using tag hint bars and context menus, see "Using tag hint bars and context menus" on page 93.

TASK 6: FORMATTING TEXT

When using Flare, it's important to understand the difference between local formatting and formatting with styles.

- **Local "inline" formatting** — Used to format characters, such as making certain words bold, underlined, or italicized in a paragraph. With this method, formatting is applied only to the selected text.

- **Styles** — Used to control formatting that you set up ahead of time in a **stylesheet**, which is simply a collection of styles. When you change a style, it changes in every place where the style was applied.

Whether you choose to use local formatting or styles to control the look of your content depends on several factors, as discussed next.

WHEN TO USE EACH METHOD

You'll practice applying styles and adding local formatting, but you should be aware of when it's appropriate to use each.

Table 2-1: When to use each formatting method

Use this option ...	When ...
Styles	• The formatting is likely to change. • The document you're creating is large and requires consistent formatting. • You need to use the same formatting in several topics or projects.
Local formatting **Note** — Using a lot of local formatting increases the size of the XML code. Your browser may take longer to display such content.	• The formatting is not likely to change. • The document you're creating is relatively small. • You don't need to use the same formatting in other topics or projects. • You need to apply the formatting to only a few areas in the content.

1. Click **Open the Text Format Toolbar** [F] in the XML Editor's toolbar. This is where local formatting is typically done.

> **Note** — You can also use the Format menu to do local formatting.

Text Format toolbar

2. Highlight **joy**.

3. Click **B** and then **I** make the selected text bold and italicized.

4. Highlight **passion**.

5. Click **B** and then **I** make the selected text bold and italicized.

6. Click anywhere in the text you formatted.

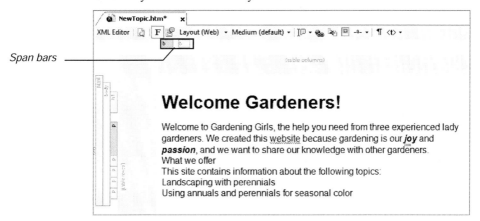

Span bars

Notice that a new type of structure bar, called span bars, has appeared along the top of the content area. **Span bars** indicate how formatting is applied where the cursor is located.

> **Note** — If you don't see span bars, click **Toggle show spans** .

Now you'll see how styles are used. Unless you specify otherwise, Flare attaches its default stylesheet, called **Style.css**, to your topic.

You can attach a different stylesheet if you create one, but since you don't have any, you'll use Flare's default stylesheet.

7. Highlight **Gardening Girls**.

8. Click the arrow in (text) on the Text Format toolbar to open a list of styles that apply to selected text.

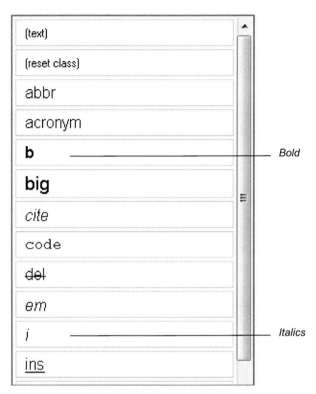

9. Select **b** (bold). The bold style is applied to the selected text.

    Next, you'll see how to apply a style to a text block.

10. Click in **What we offer**.

    > **Note** — When applying styles to a text block, click anywhere in the text block where the style will be applied. You can click anywhere in a text block and select **Format → Font** (or another option) to apply local formatting.

11. Click the arrow in [p ▾] on the Text Format toolbar to open a list of styles applicable to text blocks.

Notice that the style button on the Text Format toolbar now shows a "p" like this: instead of "text" like this: (text).

Notice also that the list of styles for text blocks is different than the list of styles for selected text. Flare shows you only those styles that apply to *either* selected text *or* a text block.

12. Select **h2** (heading level 2). Voila! The h2 style is applied to the entire text block as shown below.

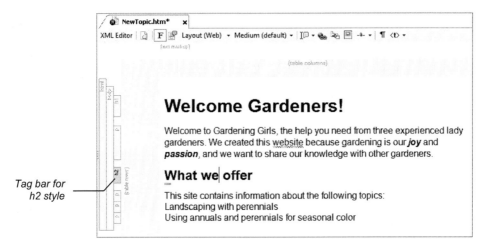

Tag bar for h2 style

Notice that Flare created a new tag bar for the h2 style as well. You can always examine the tag bar to see how formatting is applied to text blocks.

> **Best Practice** — Use styles for text blocks. It's much easier than using local formatting.

Next, you'll take a look at various layout modes in Flare.

TASK 7: VIEWING LAYOUT MODES

As you will learn in Step 5A: Create Print Output, and Step 5B: Create Online Output, you can create content specifically designed to be used online or in print. To help you see how your content will look, the XML Editor can display your content in two modes:

- **Web Layout mode** — To see how your content will look as online output (websites, Help systems, etc.) Headers and footers *are not* shown in this mode.

- **Print Layout mode** — To see how your content will look as print output (Word, PDF, FrameMaker files, etc.) Headers and footers *are* shown in this mode if you created a page layout and selected it when you set up the target currently designated as "primary."

> **Notes**
>
> To designate a target as primary, right-click the target in the Project Organizer and select **Make Primary** from the menu.
>
> Prior to Flare 4.0, the XML Editor displayed topics in Web Layout mode only.

When you're writing content for each type of output, it's helpful to see the components that make up that output—right in the editor you're working in. That's where Flare's layout modes help you out. Let's see how this works.

1. Click ▏ Layout (Web) ▾ ▏ in the toolbar above your topic. Notice that the button indicates the current mode (Web Layout).

   A message appears stating that the medium will change (to "default" for Web layout mode, and "print" for Print Layout mode). You'll learn a bit about mediums in a moment.

2. Click **OK**. The XML Editor re-displays your topic in Print Layout mode.

Print Layout mode

What are Mediums?

Mediums let you customize styles for a particular output. For example, you might want the "p" style for online output to use a sans serif font (like Verdana), which is easy to read onscreen. But for print output, you might want the "p" style to use a serif font (like Times New Roman), which is easier to see when reading printed documents.

If you want to use a medium, you must set up the medium's styles in the Stylesheet Editor and then select the applicable medium when you set up a target. The medium you select will be used for that target's output.

For now, you only need to remember that Flare automatically changes the medium when you change the layout mode.

Task 8: Creating Another Topic

As you use Flare, you'll probably have more than one topic open at once, each with its own tab in the XML Editor. But only one topic—the **active topic**—is visible at a time. To switch to a different open topic (and make it active), just click its tab.

Now you'll create a new topic (without creating its corresponding TOC entry) to see how the topic tabs work.

1. Select **Project → Add Topic**. The Add New Topic dialog opens, just as it did when you first created the project.

2. Click **Add**, then OK to confirm where the file will be copied.

    The new topic opens in its own tab and is listed in the Content Explorer to the left of the XML Editor.

Topic tabs

3. To switch between topics and make a topic active, click its tab. Try switching between topics a couple times to see how this works.

> ***Best Practice*** — Don't have more than three or four topics open at one time. Most people find it difficult to keep track of several topics at once.

TASK 9: SAVING A PROJECT

Enough practice for now. It's time to save your work.

Flare allows you to save the active topic or your entire project. You'll save your project.

1. Click **Save All** ⊞ in the Standard (top) toolbar. Notice that the topic tabs do not show asterisks, meaning that all changed content has been saved.

2. Close Flare if you're not ready to move on to Step 3: Develop Content, in this book.

> ***Best Practice*** — Use **Save All** ⊞ rather than **Save Topic** ⊟. That way, you'll be sure to save all your work before exiting.

LEARN MORE

This section provides more detail about some of the features you used during this tutorial. Appendix C: XML Editor Reference, has even more information about other XML features you might find useful, plus shortcuts and charts for quick reference when working with the XML Editor.

USING XML EDITOR TOOLBARS

The XML Editor has two local toolbars:

-   **Top toolbar** — To switch view modes and add links, cross-references, and images.

Figure 2-3:
Top toolbar

- **Bottom toolbar** — To change the magnification of the text in Web Layout mode, to page through a document in Print Layout mode, and to view structure bars.

Figure 2-4:
Bottom toolbar in Web Layout mode

Figure 2-5
Bottom toolbar in Page Layout mode

See Appendix C: XML Editor Reference, for complete list of toolbar buttons.

USING STRUCTURE BARS

Structure bars—visual cues that show the structure of a topic's tags—provide a quick and convenient way to access XML Editor features (such as inserting rows and columns in tables). Flare contains these structure bars:

- **Tag bars** — Appear to the left of the content area and show tags for each block in your topic. (The highlighted bar shows which block your cursor is in.)

Figure 2-6:
Tag bars

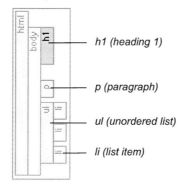

h1 (heading 1)

p (paragraph)

ul (unordered list)

li (list item)

- **Span bars** — Appear at the top of the content area and show span tags—formatting such as bold, italics, and conditional text applied directly to characters.

Figure 2-7:
Span bars

> **Note** — Figure 2-11 shows both tag and span bars in the XML Editor window.

- **Table Row bars** — Show structure bars for rows in the table in which your cursor is positioned. There is one numbered bar for each row.

Figure 2-8:
Table row
bars

- **Table Column Bars** — Show structure bars for columns in the table in which your cursor is positioned. There is one bar for each column.

Figure 2-9:
Table column
bars

Structure bar menus

Besides providing visual cues, structure bars provide menus for working with the text in your topics. Clicking a structure bar causes its menu to appear.

Figure 2-10: Menu for a tag structure bar

TOGGLING TAG AND SPAN BARS ON AND OFF

To view more of a topic, you may want to toggle tag and span bars off in the XML Editor tab for that topic. If you use them frequently, you may want to toggle them on.

> *Note* — Structure bars can be turned on for one topic and off for another.

Figure 2-11:
XML Editor tag and span bars

Span bar

Tag bars

To ...	Click ...
Toggle the tag bars on or off *Tag bars appear on the left and show tags that surround text blocks.*	
Toggle the span bars on or off *Span bars appear at the top and show character formatting, such as bold, italics, and condition tags.*	

VIEWING MARKERS

Markers are used to flag certain elements (such as index entries, bookmarks, and variables) that you've inserted into a topic. You can view or hide them by selecting **Show Markers** from the list on the **Toggle show tags** button of the XML Top toolbar.

Marker

Figure 2-12:
Bookmark marker in view

Maple Trees

The Acer Truncatum is a small maple tree that is suitable for curbside or in smaller areas, such as patios.

You'll learn more about markers later when we discuss creating an index in Step 4: Create Navigation Aids. See "Creating index entries" on page 171.

USING TAG HINT BARS AND CONTEXT MENUS

As you saw in Task 5 (Manipulating Text), Flare's XML Editor has a useful feature called **tag hint bars**. Tag hint bars open context menus, which provide quick access to features related to the selected text or to the text block your cursor is positioned within. To view the context menu, hover your cursor over the tag hint bar and click it.

The XML Editor contains two kinds of tag hint bars:

- **Red tag hint bars** — Appear at the beginning of the *selected text* and expand to provide menu options (such as copy and paste) that are applicable to selected text.

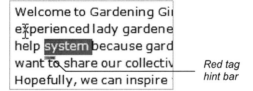

Red tag hint bar

- **Yellow tag hint bars** — Appear at the beginning of the *text block* your cursor is positioned within and provide applicable menu options (such as the ability to create a snippet from the text block).

Yellow tag hint bar

To open the context menu for the selected text:

1. Select the text to work with. A red tag hint bar appears under the first selected word.

2. Hover your cursor over the red bar to expand it. The bar changes to a flashing red rectangle.

> Welcome to Gardening Gi|
> experienced lady gardene
> help system because gard
> want share our collectiv
> Hopefully, we can inspire
> maybe help you with your

3. Click the red rectangle to open a context menu.

4. Select the desired menu option.

 To open the context menu for a text block:

1. Place your cursor anywhere within the text block you want to work with. A yellow tag hint bar appears under the first character of the first word in the block.

2. Hover your cursor over the yellow bar to expand it. The bar changes to a flashing yellow rectangle.

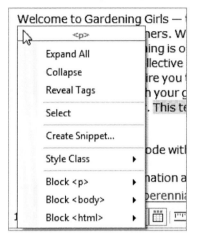

3. Click the rectangle to open a context menu.

4. Select the desired menu option.

WHAT'S NEXT?

Ready to learn more about Flare?

The next chapter, Step 3: Develop Content, describes how to develop content after you have entered or imported it. Specifically, you'll explore how to work with lists, tables, images, styles, and special symbols and characters.

Step 3: Develop Content

STEP 5: Create Output
5A: Print Output
5B: Online Output

STEP 4:
Create
Nav Aids

STEP 3:
Develop
Content

STEP 2:
Learn the
XML Editor

STEP 1:
Get Started

In this chapter ...

- ➤ Copy text into a topic
- ➤ Delete a topic
- ➤ Work with lists
- ➤ Work with tables
- ➤ Work with images
- ➤ Add symbols and special characters
- ➤ Format your content

OVERVIEW

Throughout this book, you'll see **content** and **topic** used often. Let's take a moment to review what these terms mean:

- A **topic** is the "box" in which content is stored. Each topic is a file (with an .htm extension) that conforms to the XML specification.

- **Content** is various types of information contained in a topic, such as text, tables, lists, images, links, and multimedia.

A Flare **project** is simply a collection of topics and related files, which are stored in **project folders**.

In this chapter, you'll learn how to:

- Copy and paste content into a topic (without importing it)

- Delete a topic

- Add lists, tables, images, and special characters to topics

- Format your content

Your content can be new or imported (see Appendix B: Import Content, for more about importing content). This chapter does *not* describe how to create navigational aids (links, TOCs, indexes) that point to topics. We'll cover those in Step 4: Create Navigation Aids.

Let's begin by learning how to copy text into a topic.

> ***Note*** — To learn how to create new topics, see "Adding a topic" on page 45.

COPYING AND PASTING TEXT INTO A TOPIC

There may be times when you have small pieces of text you want to insert into topics. Copying and pasting is the fastest and easiest way to do it. This method works well for small blocks of text that will not become standalone topics.

Flare's paste feature is smart! It lets you decide what format to use when pasting the text.

To copy and paste text into a topic:

1. Open the Flare topic you want to paste the text into.

2. Select the source text and press **CTRL + C** to copy it (from Word, FrameMaker, another Flare topic, or any other word processing application).

3. Place your cursor where you want to insert the text and press **CTRL + V**. If you're pasting content from another application, the Paste Text dialog opens and shows a preview of the text you are pasting; otherwise, the content is pasted immediately.

4.　In the Options section, choose how you want the text pasted (as a paragraph, paragraph block, list, table, etc.). To the right of your choice, select the style to apply to the text (if applicable).

5.　Click **Paste** to paste the text.

DELETING A TOPIC

You can delete a topic from your project, but use caution when doing so, as other topics or project files might link to that topic.

> ### Important
>
> Before deleting a topic, we recommend that you save a backup copy of your project. Then check for and remove links to that topic.
>
> When you delete a topic, its index markers are also deleted.

CHECKING FOR LINKS TO A TOPIC

Use the following procedure to check for links to a topic.

 To check for links:

1.　Open the Content Explorer.

2.　Right-click the topic and select **Show Dependencies** from the menu. The List Dependencies dialog opens.

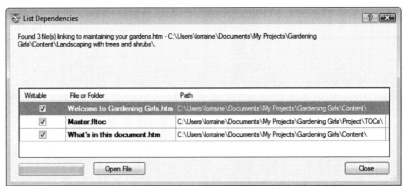

3. To open a linked file, select the file and click **Open File**. You can then change or remove the link in the file. (Opening a file closes the List Dependencies dialog.)

4. Click **Close** to close the dialog.

DELETING A TOPIC

> **Best Practice** — Before deleting a topic, save a backup copy of your project. Then check for and remove links to that topic.

Use the following procedure to delete a topic from your project.

 To delete a topic:

1. Make sure that the Flare project is open and the Content Explorer is in view.

2. Do one of the following:

   - Select the topic in the Content Explorer and select **Edit** → **Delete**.

   - Right-click the topic and select **Delete** from the menu.

3. Select **OK** to confirm the deletion.

   If the topic has links to other files, such as links to other topics or a TOC, the Link Update dialog opens.

Name of the file you are deleting

Path to the linked file

4. Do one of the following:

To ...	Do this ...
Delete the topic and remove all links to it	Click **Remove Links**.
	Note
	Removing the link to a TOC creates an unlinked TOC item. *Removing* the link to another topic leaves the unlinked text of the link in the other topic.
Delete the topic without removing links to it	Click **Do Not Remove Links**.
	Note
	Leaving the link to a TOC or other topic creates a broken link in the TOC or topic.
Cancel without deleting this topic	Click **Cancel**.

If you selected **Remove Links** or **Do Not Remove Links**, the topic is deleted from your project.

5. Click **Save All** to save your work.

WORKING WITH LISTS

As with most word processing programs, Flare lets you add various types of lists to your content, including:

- Single-level lists

- Multi-level lists

- Numbered lists, sequenced by numbers or letters

- Bulleted lists

You can also add items to lists, rearrange and sort them, and merge lists.

CREATING A LIST

Before you create a list, you should know what your choices are.

> ## DECISION TIME!
>
> ✓ Do you want to create a bulleted list or a numbered list?
>
> ✓ If you want a bulleted list, what type of bullets do you want (black circle, empty circle, or square)?
>
> ✓ If you want a numbered list, what type of numbers do you want (Arabic, lower-case alphabetic, upper-case alphabetic, lower-case roman numerals, or upper-case roman numerals)?

> **Note** — In the XML world, bulleted lists are also called **unordered lists** because the order of the items *is not* significant. Numbered lists, such as step-by-step procedures, are also called **ordered lists** because the order of list items *is* important.

Creating a single-level list

Use this procedure to create single-level bulleted or numbered lists.

To create a single-level list:

1. In the desired topic, place your cursor where you want the list to start.

2. If the Text Format toolbar is not in view, click **Open the Text Format Toolbar** **F** in the XML Editor's toolbar.

3. Click the list button's right arrow.

> **Note** — The appearance of the list button changes to reflect the type of list you last chose. For example here are just a few possibilities for the appearance of the list button: ▤ ▾ ▤ ▾ ▤ ▾

If the list type you want is the one last used, you can click the button instead of the right arrow and skip Step 4, next.

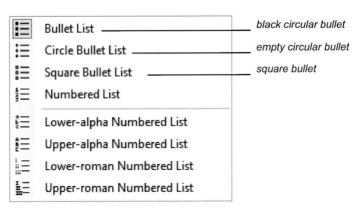

4. Select the type of list you want to create.

5. Type the text of the list item.

6. At the end of the line for the first list item, press **ENTER** (only once). A second list item is created.

> **Tip** — If you press **ENTER** more than once, Flare thinks that you're done creating the list. Instead of giving you more list items, it gives you paragraphs in which to type text. If this happens, simply place your cursor at the end of the last list item you typed, and press **ENTER**. Your list will continue where you left off.

7. Continue adding items if desired (Steps 5 and 6 above).

> **Note** — You can also create a list by a) typing the text first, selecting it, and then selecting the type of list to apply to the text or b) placing your cursor where you want to start the list, selecting **Format → List**, and selecting the type of list.

Creating a multi-level list

You've just seen how to create a simple one-level numbered or bulleted list. But not all lists are simple. For example, if you're writing step-by-step instructions, you might need to break out one step into a series of smaller tasks—each one a step.

Example of a multi-level list

1. First numbered item
   a. 1st second-level item
   b. 2nd second-level item
2. Second numbered item
3. Third numbered item

Use the following procedure to create a multi-level list with Flare's indenting feature.

> **Note** — To learn how to create a multi-level list by using styles, search on "creating multi-level lists" in the Flare Help system.

To create a multi-level list:

1. Create a single-level list that contains all of the items.

2. Indent the desired items by clicking **Indent Items**.

3. Apply the desired list type to the indented items. (Click the list button's right arrow and select the list type.)

   > **Note** — You can also place your cursor where you want to start the list and select **Format → List**. Then select the type of list.

CHANGING LISTS

Flare includes many options for changing lists, such as:

- Rearranging items

- Sorting items

- Assigning a different number to an item

- Merging two or more lists into one

The **Drop down menu of assorted list actions** button lists what you can do with lists. Next, you'll read about some of the more frequently used options.

Figure 3-1:
*Menu of
assorted list
actions*

Merge With Previous List

Merge With Next List

Sort List

Reverse List

Unbind List

Continue Sequence

List Start #:   1

Item #:   1

Move Up

Move Down

Make Simple Item(s)

Make Paragraph Item(s)

Rearranging lists

You can easily rearrange the items in a list by moving them up or down.

To rearrange a list:

1. Place your cursor within the list item to be moved.

2. Click **Drop down menu of assorted list actions** .

   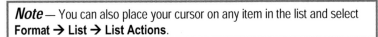

   Note — You can also place your cursor on any item in the list and select **Format → List → List Actions**.

3. Select **Move Up** or **Move Down**.

4. Continue moving items until the list is arranged to your liking.

Sorting a list

List items can be sorted in ascending order based on the text contained in each list item. For example, suppose you have the following list items:

1. AAA
2. SSS
3. MM
4. MMMMM
5. BB
6. FFF

A sorted list would look like this.

1. AAA
2. BB
3. FFF
4. MM
5. MMMMM
6. SSS

Notice that the sequence numbers don't stay with the text. In this case, the list started with number 1 and it still does, even after being sorted.

To sort a list:

1. Place your cursor anywhere in the list.

2. Click **Drop down menu of assorted list actions** .

    > **Note** — You can also place your cursor on any item in the list and select **Format → List → List Actions.**

3. Select **Sort List**.

    The list items are sorted in ascending alphabetical order.

    > **Note** — To switch the order from ascending to descending or vice versa, select **Reverse List** from the List Actions menu.

Re-numbering a list

Flare lets you assign a starting sequence number to any item in an ordered list. Items that follow that item will automatically be re-numbered (unless you have set their starting sequence number.)

You can also reset the sequence number of an item. Resetting assigns the next number in the sequence (based on the previous list item).

The **Drop down menu of assorted list actions** contains three options for setting and resetting sequence numbers in ordered lists.

Figure 3-2:
Options for
setting and
resetting
sequence
numbers

Continue Sequence

List Start #:   1

Item #:   1

We'll talk about these options next.

To assign a sequence number to the first item in a list:

1. Place your cursor on any item in the list.

2. Click **Drop down menu of assorted list actions**.

   > **Note** — You can also place your cursor on any item in the list and select **Format → List → List Actions**.

3. Select a starting number by clicking the up or down arrow next to **List Start** #, then click the blue arrow on the right.

List Start #:   1   ——— *Then click here.*

Click to set the
starting number.

The first item in the list is set to the starting number you selected, and the remaining list items are re-sequenced in ascending one-unit increments. For example, if you set the first item to 20, the remaining items will be numbered starting at 21.

To assign a sequence number to any item in a list:

1. Place your cursor on the list item whose number you want to set.

> **Note** — You can also place your cursor on any item in the list and select **Format → List → List Actions.**

2. Click **Drop down menu of assorted list actions** .

Item #:   9

> **Note** — Notice that our cursor was on the list item whose number is currently "9" and "**Item # 9**" appears in the List Actions menu. (Don't get confused between an item's sequence number and its placement in the list. Just because its sequence number is 9 does not mean that it's the ninth item in the list.)

3. Select a starting number for that item by clicking the up or down arrow next to **Item** #, then click the blue arrow on the right.

Click to set the starting number.   *Then click here.*

Item #:   9

The item is set to the starting number you selected and the items that follow it are re-sequenced in ascending order.

Merging lists

If your topic has lists that need to be combined, you can easily merge them. But before merging them, the lists must be consecutive (in other words, you cannot combine lists that have non-list elements between them). Make sure you delete any non-list items before trying to merge two lists or move the second list so it immediately follows the first.

> **Tip** — To merge three lists, just merge the first two into one, and then merge that list with the next one.

Can I merge different types of lists?

Yes, you can merge two lists that are of different types. For example, you can merge a numbered list with a bulleted list. When Flare combines the lists, it applies the list type from the first list to the second list.

Let's say the first list looks like this:

1. first numbered item
2. second numbered item
3. third numbered item

And the second list looks like this:

- first bullet item
- second bullet item
- third bullet item

After you combine them, the list will look like this:

1. first numbered item
2. second numbered item
3. third numbered item
4. first bullet item
5. second bullet item
6. third bullet item

What happens to the sequence numbers when I merge lists?

As you can see from the example, if the first list is an ordered list, Flare automatically applies the next number in sequence to the first item in the second list. So the result is a seamless, perfectly sequenced group of list items.

To merge two lists:

1. In the topic that contains the two lists, verify that there are no non-list elements between the two lists.

   > **Note** — You might have to remove the text that's between the lists or copy the second list and paste it immediately after the first list. (To delete text, see "Deleting text" on page 297.)

2. Place your cursor on any item in either list.

3. Click **Drop down menu of assorted list actions** .

> **Note** — You can also place your cursor on any item in the list and select **Format → List → List Actions**.

4. Select **Merge With Next List** or **Merge With Previous List** (depending on which list — the first or second — your cursor is located in).

WORKING WITH TABLES

Tables allow you to organize information in a graphical format that is easier for most people to read than blocks of text. Tables consist of cells (the intersection of rows and columns), which can contain text and images.

You can format tables with styles from a table stylesheet or with local formatting. Local formatting (sometimes called inline formatting) means applying formats such as borders and shading to cells in a table without using styles. See "Formatting tables" on page 115 for more information.

> **Note** — For new users, we recommend using local formatting or using table styles as is until you're better acquainted with Flare. Then change table styles as you prefer.

When you create a table, you'll use the Insert Table dialog to set up the table's characteristics (number of columns, number of rows, table caption etc.).

THE INSERT TABLE DIALOG

The Insert Table dialog (Figure 3-3) contains options for adding a table to a topic. It contains two tabs: **Basic** and **Borders**.

The Basic tab

The Basic tab contains options for setting the size of the table, its caption, its style, and how columns are sized.

Figure 3-3:
Insert Table
dialog,
Basic tab

Table 3-1:	In this section ...	Do the following ...
Options on the Insert Table dialog, Basic tab	Table Size	Select the size of the table: • **Number of columns** — Select or type the number of columns. • **Number of rows** — Select or type the number of rows. • **Number of header rows** — Select or type the number of header rows. • **Number of footer rows** — Select or type the number of footer rows. (Helpful for entering footnotes about a table's contents.)

Table 3-1:
(Cont.)

In this section ...	Do the following ...
AutoFit Behavior	Select the method for adjusting column width:

■ AutoFit to contents automatically adjusts the column width to fit the size of the text it contains and wraps the contents to fit the window size.

> *Note* — For best results, we recommend that you use the **AutoFit to contents** option.

■ AutoFit to window automatically adjusts the column width to fit the window size.

■ In the drop-down box to the right, if you enter a percentage, the table will fill up to that percentage of the window width (even if it means padding the end of a cell with blanks). If you select automatic, Flare will not pad the cells with blanks in order to fit the window width. If you set a length, the table will not resize wider than the number you set, regardless of the window width.

■ Fixed column width sets all columns to a fixed width, but automatically adjusts the column widths equally to fit the window if resized. To set the column width, open the list to the right of this field, click its down arrow and set the "length."

> *Note* — In the two drop-down boxes to the right, **default** returns to the default, which is "not set."

In this section ...	Do the following ...
Align	Select the table alignment: Left (default), Center, or Right.
Table Caption	If you want to add a table caption, type it here and select the position of the caption (Above table or Below table).

> *Note* — If you choose "Below," Internet Explorer might put the caption above the table instead of below.

Table 3-1: (Cont.)	**In this section ...**	**Do the following ...**
	Table Style	If you want to use a table stylesheet for this table, select it from the Table Style list. Options include:
		■ **Add** — If the stylesheet you want to use is not listed under Table Styles, click this button to add the table stylesheet to the project. The stylesheet appears in the Table Style list. This option adds the style to the project and to the table you are creating.
		■ **Print Style** — Click this button to select a table stylesheet to use for print output only.
		■ **CSS Class** — (*An advanced feature*) Allows you to format the text in your table by selecting a style class from the topic's stylesheet (for example, Styles.css).
	Preview	Select to preview the table's style and the choices you made on this tab (such as table size and caption).

The Borders tab

The Borders tab contains options for applying and formatting borders around the cells of your table.

Figure 3-4:
Insert Table dialog, Borders tab

Table 3-2:
Options on the Insert Table dialog, Borders tab

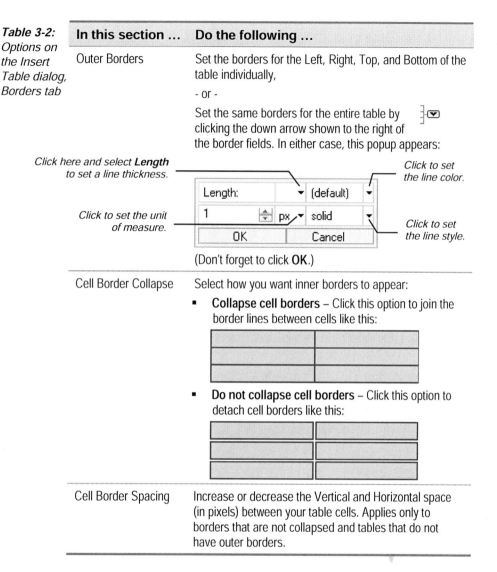

In this section ...	Do the following ...
Outer Borders	Set the borders for the Left, Right, Top, and Bottom of the table individually, - or - Set the same borders for the entire table by clicking the down arrow shown to the right of the border fields. In either case, this popup appears:

*Click here and select **Length** to set a line thickness.*

Click to set the unit of measure.

Click to set the line color.

Click to set the line style.

(Don't forget to click **OK**.)

Cell Border Collapse	Select how you want inner borders to appear: ▪ **Collapse cell borders** – Click this option to join the border lines between cells like this: ▪ **Do not collapse cell borders** – Click this option to detach cell borders like this:
Cell Border Spacing	Increase or decrease the Vertical and Horizontal space (in pixels) between your table cells. Applies only to borders that are not collapsed and tables that do not have outer borders.

FORMATTING TABLES

Flare gives you options for formatting tables, but you must decide how you want to manage the formats applied to the tables.

> **DECISION TIME!**
>
> ✓   Do you want to use local formatting or table styles?
>
> To answer this question, you need to consider the following:
>
> ✓   Will you be creating many tables in different topics?
>
> ✓   Do you want all tables in your project to look the same (have the same format, not necessarily the same number of columns)?
>
> If you answer "yes" to these last two questions, use table styles.

So which option are you going to choose? Here's what we suggest.

Our recommendation

Styles are complex concepts to understand. For your first Flare project, we recommend that you keep things simple by using local formatting (page 134) or use table styles without changing them.

However, we also recommend that later—once you're more comfortable and skilled with using Flare—you learn about table styles and try changing them to meet your needs, especially if you have many tables that require the same formatting. It will be worth the investment of time when you're ready to take on the learning challenge. We briefly discuss how to apply table styles on page 138.

> **Note** — For more detailed information about styles, see the *MadCap Flare Styles Guide*, available by selecting **Help → Guides → Styles Guide**.

For now, let's move on so you can see how to include a table in a topic.

ADDING A TABLE

Follow these instructions to add a table to the active topic.

🎁 To add a table:

1.   Place your cursor where you want to insert the table.

2.   Select **Table → Insert → Table**. The Insert Table dialog opens (Figure 3-3).

3. Fill in the fields on each tab of the Insert Table dialog. For descriptions of the fields, see Table 3-1and Table 3-2.

> *Tip* — You can easily change a table's characteristics later by selecting **Table → Table Properties,** or by clicking the table's structure bar and selecting **Table Properties** from the structure bar menu.

4. When finished, click **OK**.

You now have a table that is ready for content. To type text in the table's cells, simply position your cursor in a cell and type. You can also add images and links.

SHOWING GRID LINES

Table gridlines help you to see where table cells are. You can easily turn gridlines on or off as needed.

Grid lines appear in the XML Editor only; they do not show up in your output. (If you want borders around cells, see "Formatting tables" on page 115.)

To show grid lines:

- Select **Table → Show Gridlines**.

USING TABLE STRUCTURE BARS

With Flare's XML Editor you can show or hide structure bars that represent your table's rows and columns.

- **Table Row Bars** — Appear to the left of your topic. There is one numbered bar for each row in your table.

- **Table Column Bars** — Appear above your topic. There is one bar, labeled with the column's width, for each column in your table.

Table row and column bars make it easy to insert, delete, and resize rows and columns in your tables. You can also use Flare's **Table** menu to delete rows and columns.

To show table row and column bars:

- Click anywhere within the table and do the following:

Click ...	To show ...
	Column bars
	Row bars

Here's a table with row and column bars in view.

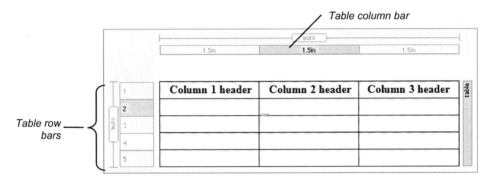

Table column bar

Table row bars

Structure bars have menus with choices that are meaningful based on your cursor location. For more information about structure bars and their menus, see "Using structure bars" on page 89.

To select a row or column:

1. View the table row or table column bars.

2. Select the desired row or column bar and choose **Select**.

> **Note** — You can also place your cursor in the desired row or column and select **Table → Select → Column or Row**.

To select the entire table:

1. Place your cursor anywhere in the table. A table bar appears to the right of the table.

2. Click the table bar and choose **Select**.

> *Note* — You can also place your cursor in the table and select **Table →
> Select → Table**.

INSERTING ROWS AND COLUMNS

Follow these instructions to insert rows and columns in tables.

🎩 To insert a row:

1. If not in view, show table row bars (see page 117).

2. Click the bar for the row after which (or before which) you want
    to insert a row.

3. From the menu, select **Insert New (Above)** or **Insert New
    (Below)**.

    A blank row is inserted either above or below the row whose bar
    you clicked.

> *Tips*
>
> You can also place your cursor where you want to add the row and select
> **Table → Rows Above** or **Rows Below**.
>
> To insert a row at the end of the table, place your cursor at the end of the
> table's last cell and press **TAB**.

🎩 To insert a column:

1. If not in view, show table column bars (see page 117).

2. Click the bar for the column after which (or before which) you
    want to insert a column.

3. From the menu, select **Insert New (Left)** or **Insert New (Right)**.

    A blank column is inserted to the left or right of the column
    whose bar you clicked.

> *Note* — You can also place your cursor where you want to add a column
> and select **Table → Insert → Columns to the Left** or **Columns to the
> Right**.

DELETING ROWS AND COLUMNS

Follow these instructions to delete rows and columns from tables.

To delete a row or column:

1. If not in view, show the row or column structure bars (see page 117).

2. Click the structure bar of the row or column you want to delete.

3. From the menu, select **Delete**.

> **Note** — You can also place your cursor in the row or column you want to delete and select **Table → Delete → Columns or Rows**.

RESIZING ROWS AND COLUMNS

Follow these instructions to resize rows and columns in tables.

To resize a row:

1. If not in view, show the row structure bars (see page 117).

2. Hover your cursor over the *row number* of the structure bar for the row you want to resize until you see a vertical double-arrow.

3. Drag the arrow to change the row's height.

Flare shows the height of the row in pixels, which changes dynamically as you drag the row. When you stop dragging, the structure bar shows the new height in pixels.

> **Note** — You can also click the row's structure bar and use the resize arrows in the menu to set the size. (Click the blue arrow when done.)

To resize a column:

1. If not in view, show the column structure bars (see page 117).

2. Hover your cursor over the line between the structure bars to the right of the column you want to resize until you see a horizontal double-arrow.

3. Drag the arrow to change the column's width.

    Flare shows the width of the column in pixels, which changes dynamically as you drag the column. When you stop dragging, the structure bar shows the new width in pixels.

    > *Note* — You can also resize a column by clicking the column's structure bar whose menu shows the current size. Use the resize arrows in the menu to set the size. (Click the blue arrow when done.)   `1.50  ▲▼  in  ▼  ↵`

MOVING ROWS AND COLUMNS

You can move rows and columns in your table by dragging and dropping. Here's how to do it.

To move a row:

1. If not in view, show the row structure bars (see page 117).

2. Hover your cursor over the structure bar of the row to be moved until the mouse pointer turns into an arrow and a rectangle.

3. Drag the row and drop it when the arrow points to the place you want to move it to.

Here's the result after moving the sample row.

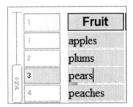

To move a column:

1. If not in view, show the column structure bars (see page 117).

2. Hover your cursor over the structure bar of the column to be moved until the mouse pointer turns into an arrow with a rectangle.

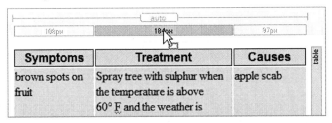

3. Drag the column and drop it when the arrow points to the place you want to move it to.

Here's the result after moving the sample column.

WORKING WITH IMAGES

Flare lets you add images, such as photographs, screen captures, and illustrations, to your topics.

The image can be a vector or raster file in any of these formats: BMP, EMF, EXPS, GIF, HDP, JPG, JPEG, PNG, SWF, TIF, TIFF, WDP, WMF, XAML, and XPS.

> **Best Practice** — Create your images in their final size if possible, to avoid any issues with resizing.

WHERE ARE IMAGES STORED?

By default, Flare stores images in the Resources\Images folder of the Content Explorer. If the image you want to add is not already in this folder, Flare puts it there when you add the image to your topic.

> **Tip** — If desired, you can copy images to the Resources\Images folder from Windows Explorer before you're ready to add them to topics.

You can add an image from the Resources\Images folder to any topic in your project. By reusing images, you'll keep your project size smaller, since Flare keeps only one copy of each image in this folder.

FLARE MANAGES IMAGE FILE CHANGES

When you add an image to a topic, Flare keeps a link to that image. If you later change its name in the Resources\Images folder—even from Windows Explorer—Flare handles the name change without any further action on your part. Your link between the file and the image in your topic will not be broken! The Content Explorer's Resources\Images folder shows the new name, and the link in the topic is also correct. How cool is that?

And here's another feature that we think is pretty neat. If you edit the image using an external application and replace it (keeping the file name the same), the image in your topic is automatically updated.

An example

Let's say that you copied a photograph called "MyPhoto.jpg" to the Resources\Images folder, inserted it into a topic, and then noticed that the photo has red-eye. To fix it, you can just open the photo in your photo editing software, remove the red-eye, and re-save the photo to the Resources\Images folder. When you view the photo in your topic you'll see that the red-eye is gone!

ADDING AN IMAGE

Follow these instructions to add an image to a topic and to the open project.

To add an image to a topic:

1. Place your cursor where you want to insert the image in the topic.

2. Select **Insert → Picture**. The Insert Picture dialog opens.

3. Select an image to insert by doing one of the following:

   ▪ Click **Browse** to navigate to it.
     – or –

   ▪ Select one of the options shown under Choose Source and
     then select the picture from the list on the right.

   A preview of the image appears at the bottom of the dialog.

4. (*Optional*) Type a screen tip (text that appears when you hover
   your cursor over the image in the built output).

5. (*Optional*) Type alternate text if you need to produce output that
   is compliant with Section 508 of the United States Rehabilitation
   Act. Alternate text could be useful for visually impaired
   individuals who might use screen readers. (For more
   information, search for "Section 508" in the Flare Help system.)

6. Click **OK**.

   If the image is not already in your project, a dialog confirms that
   the image will be copied to your project.

7. Click **OK** to copy the image to your project.

   The picture is added to your topic and to your project's
   Resources\Images folder (if not already there).

> ***Note*** — Don't forget to save your project! Select **File** ➔ **Save All** or click
>
> **Save All** 🖼 to save the topic with the image you added to the
> Resources\Images folder.

ADDING SCREEN CAPTURES FROM MADCAP CAPTURE

If you have MadCap Capture™, Flare lets you add and edit screen
captures directly from Capture. Capture stores graphic elements in
layers, so you can capture a screen shot and add graphic elements
(like callouts) to it. To find out more, see your MadCap Capture
Help system.

RESIZING AN IMAGE

After you add images to your topics, you have a few ways to resize them. Just like with tables, you can resize an image locally (within a topic) or you can control an image's size with styles.

So which method is right for you? Here's what we suggest.

Do this ...	When ...
Resize images locally	You have only a few images in a topic or project or image sizing in your project doesn't need to be consistent
Resize images with a stylesheet	You have many images and need consistent image sizing throughout your project

Our recommendation

Because styles can be overwhelming, for your first Flare project, we recommend that you use local formatting. However, later—once you're farther along on the learning curve—we suggest that you learn about using styles to resize images, especially if you have many images that need to be sized the same.

In this section, you'll learn the two ways to resize images locally.

Resizing and image quality

Flare supports images in vector or raster format. The type of format determines if image quality is affected when images are resized or cropped.

- **Vector images** — Can easily be resized without any loss of quality. (Vector images are composed of points connected by lines and curves that form objects that are defined mathematically.)

- **Raster (bitmap) images** — Can be resized, but when you enlarge them, the image might become blurry because the dots move farther apart. (Raster images are composed of a collection of dots, called pixels, arranged in a grid pattern called a bitmap.) You can however, crop a raster image with no loss of quality.

Digital cameras and scanners generally create files in raster formats, such as JPG, BMP, TIF, TIFF, GIF, and PNG files. Some illustration applications (such as CorelDRAW®) create files in vector format; others (such as Adobe Photoshop®) create files in raster format.

> ***Best Practice*** — Create your images in their final size if possible, to avoid any issues with resizing.

To resize an image locally by using a mouse:

1. Hover your cursor over the image to be resized. A button appears in the image's lower right corner.

2. Drag the button diagonally *toward* the center of the image (to reduce image size) or diagonally *away from* the center of the image (to enlarge the image).

To resize an image locally by using properties:

1. In the XML Editor, right-click the image to be resized.

2. Select **Object** from the menu. The Media Properties dialog opens.

3.　On the Size tab, set image sizes as follows:

To ...	Do this ...
Set an exact image size	In the Size section, set the Width or Height and unit of measure. To maintain an image's aspect ratio (keep it in proportion), either set the image to the desired Width (select **Length** to do this) and select **Automatic** for the Height, or vice versa.

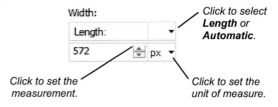

To ...	Do this ...
Set a minimum image size	In the Minimum Size section, set the minimum Length and unit of measure. To maintain an image's aspect ratio (keep it in proportion), set either the Width or the Height, but not both.

> **Note** — If the original image is *smaller* than the measurement you set, Flare enlarges the image. If the original image is *larger*, Flare doesn't change the image size.

Set a maximum image size	In the Maximum Size section, set the maximum Length and unit of measure. To maintain an image's aspect ratio (keep it in proportion), set either the Width or the Height, but not both.

> **Note** — If the original image is *larger* than the measurement you set, Flare reduces the image size. If the original image is *smaller*, Flare doesn't change the image size.

> **Important** — If you set Size tab options only, those settings will be used for both online and print output. If you set options on the Print Size tab also, then its options will be used for print output and Size tab options will be used for online output.

4. If you want the image to be one size for online output and a different size for print output, click the **Print Size** tab to set the image size for print output only. (The **Size** tab settings will then be used for online output only.)

   Use the chart above to set the options for the **Print Size** tab.

5. Click **OK**. The image is resized according to the size(s) you entered.

ADDING SYMBOLS AND SPECIAL CHARACTERS

To add symbols and special characters:

1. Place your cursor where you want to insert the special character.

2. Do one of the following:

    -   To insert the default quick character, click the **Quick Character** button.

    -   To select a different character to insert, click the down arrow on the **Quick Character** button and select the symbol or character from the list.

SETTING THE DEFAULT QUICK CHARACTER

To set the default quick character:

1. Click the down arrow on the **Quick Character** button and select **Select 'Quick Character'** from the list. The Quick Character dialog opens.

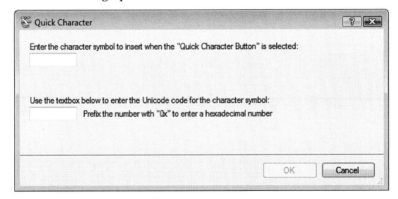

2. In the first box of the Quick Character dialog, type the character to be inserted *or* in the second box, type the Unicode code for the character or symbol you want to be the default quick character.

FORMATTING YOUR CONTENT

Formatting makes your content look better. For example, you can make your content pop by giving it a background color or changing the color of your text. Even a few changes make a big difference!

Typically, you'll want to use different font sizes for different types of headings. And for your body text, you'll likely want a font that is smaller than the font you use for headings. Actually, we can't think of a good reason *not* to format your content.

When you create topics from a Flare template, Flare's **Styles.css** stylesheet is automatically attached (more about stylesheets coming up.) Your topics will have some styles applied, as shown in Figure 3-5.

Figure 3-5:
Topic with
default
styles

Welcome

Welcome Gardeners! We developed this site because gardening is our joy and our passion, and we want to share with you our collective knowledge.

By creating this site we hope to give you the help you need so your gardens can flourish. We hope that we can inspire you to try new plants or designs, and maybe help you with your gardening questions and problems along the way.

By changing the formatting, you can add eye-catching touches such as those shown in Figure 3-6.

Figure 3-6:
Topic with
color, italics,
bold added

Welcome

Welcome Gardeners! We developed this site because gardening is our *joy* and our *passion*, and we want to share with you our collective knowledge.

By creating this site we hope to give you the help you need so your gardens can flourish. We hope that we can inspire you to try new plants or designs, and maybe help you with your gardening questions and problems along the way.

WAYS TO FORMAT CONTENT

As mentioned earlier in this book, there are two ways to apply formats to your content:

- With local formatting
- With styles from a stylesheet

We'll cover both of these methods in this section.

WHAT'S THE DIFFERENCE?

Both styles and local formatting can be applied to selected text or to a text block. The difference between them is how the formatting is applied and how it's maintained.

Local formatting

Local (inline) formatting is applied by clicking a toolbar button (bold, italics, etc.) **or by setting properties** (bold, font, indentation, etc.) for the text or text block. If you want to change the format later, you have to find the text that you applied it to. If you applied the same format in many places (in one or more topics), this could be a daunting task. (For instructions, see "Applying local formatting" on page 133.)

Formatting with styles

A style's formatting is applied by selecting a style from a stylesheet (a collection of styles). A style is a named set of characteristics (formats) that are contained in a file called a cascading stylesheet (CSS). It's called "cascading" because the styles flow down from higher-level "parent" elements (such as body tags) to lower-level "child" element (such as paragraph tags). Child elements inherit the formatting of their parent elements.

> **Note** — Cascading stylesheets apply to more than Flare; they're used to format HTML and XML documents too. But our focus here is Flare, not cascading stylesheets in general, so we'll talk about stylesheets in the context of Flare only.

By applying styles to text throughout your project, you can give your project a consistent look that is easy to change. Best of all, if you need to change the formatting, you change it in one place—in the stylesheet—and the change is propagated to every piece of text or text block to which the style is applied.

LOCAL FORMATTING VS. STYLES: WHICH TO USE

Both local formatting and styles are useful in different circumstances. Here's some information to help you decide which to use when.

Table 3-3: When to use local formatting vs. styles

Use this option ...	When ...
Local formatting	• You want to apply the format to only one or two areas of text in one topic. (Applying lots of local formats increases the size of the underlying XML code, which means the browser might take longer to display the content for WebHelp.) • You don't need to use the same formatting in other topics or projects. • The formatting is not likely to change.
Style from a CSS	• You want your topics to have a consistent appearance. • You want to use the same formatting in many places in the same or different topics. • You want to use the same formatting in different projects. • The formatting is likely to change.

APPLYING LOCAL FORMATTING

You can apply formatting within a text block or to an entire block of text by using the Text Format toolbar or by changing the properties of the text you select or text block your cursor is in.

To apply local formatting to selected text:

1. Select the text to apply the format to.

2. Do one of the following:

   - From the Text Format toolbar, select the toolbar button for the format you want (font, point size, bold, italics, color, background color).

   - Change the properties of the text by selecting **Format →
Font**. Then select the font, size, color, style (bold, italics), background color as desired.

 To apply local formatting to a text block (paragraph):

1. Place your cursor anywhere in the text block you want to format.

2. Select **Format → Paragraph**. Then change the properties as desired on the various tabs of the Paragraph Properties dialog.

APPLYING LOCAL FORMATTING TO TABLES

If you select "default" for the table style when you insert a table in a topic, your table will be formatted like this:

Figure 3-7:
Default
table style

Most likely, you'll want to format the table for maximum readability (as well as for aesthetics). You can apply formatting (color, borders, spacing) to tables by using buttons on the Text Format toolbar or by changing the properties of a table's text. For example, maybe you'd like to add color to the background or to the text of your table's cells; or maybe you'd like the table header to be distinct from the table rows.

Here's an example of how you can dress up the table shown in Figure 3-7.

Figure 3-8:
Table after
formatting
with
color

Use this procedure to format tables with local formatting.

To apply local formatting to a table:

- Set the formatting for the text in a table's cells as described in this table:

To ...	Do this ...
Apply a background color to text	Select the text to apply the color to, select **Format → Background Color**, and select a color from the color chart.
Format text in one cell	Click inside the cell you want to format, select **Format → Font**, and select the font characteristics (font, size, style, text color, background color, effects) from the Font Properties dialog. Then select **OK**.
Format text in cells	Select the text to format, select **Format → Font**, and select the font characteristics (font, size, style, text color, background color, effects) from the Font Properties dialog. Then select **OK**.
Do any of the following for one or more cells: ■ Align the text ■ Set the first line indentation ■ Set line spacing ■ Set borders ■ Set spacing around cell text (padding) ■ Set hyphenation	To format one cell, click inside the cell to be formatted. To format contiguous cells, select the cells. Then select **Format → Cell**, and select the paragraph characteristics (space before and after, borders) from the Cell Properties dialog. Then select **OK**.

APPLYING STYLES FROM A STYLESHEET

Flare projects use two types of stylesheets:

- **Topic stylesheets** — Used to format content (other than tables) in your topics.

- **Table stylesheets** — Used to format the spacing, borders, and shading of tables in your topics.

Flare comes packaged with one topic stylesheet (**Styles)** and four table stylesheets (**Basic, Columns, Inner, Rows**). A Flare project can have multiple stylesheets of each type.

In this book, we describe how to apply styles from a topic stylesheet to text in a topic and how to apply table styles to tables.

> **Note** — Topic stylesheets are stored in the Resources\Stylesheets folder of the Content Explorer. Table stylesheets are stored in the Resources\TableStyles folder of the Content Explorer.

Figure 3-9:
The Styles Stylesheet in the Resources \Stylesheet folder

When you create a new Flare project, Flare automatically makes **Styles** the default topic stylesheet for the project. When you create a topic for that project, Flare automatically attaches the project's default stylesheet to that topic. So, styles from the default Flare stylesheet are automatically available for your use.

However, Flare does *not* automatically attach table stylesheets to projects. When you create a table, you can add one or more factory table stylesheets to your project, which copies them to the Resources\TableStyles folder of the Content Explorer.

Our recommendation

There is much you can do with styles and stylesheets. For example, you can create your own stylesheets and styles, and change them as desired.

> **Important** — If you choose to change a stylesheet, be sure to select the medium whose styles you want to change in the Stylesheet Editor. If you don't see your style changes applied in your topic, you might have changed the styles in a different medium than the one you intended to change.

We recommend that to begin, you simply use the styles that Flare provides. Adding and changing cascading stylesheets are beyond the scope of a book for new users. (The *MadCap Flare Styles Guide*, which became available with Flare version 4, logs in at almost 400 pages!)

Applying styles to text

There are different ways to apply a style to text in a topic. You can use the styles list on the Text Format toolbar, the Style window, the Floating Style Picker, or tag structure bars. We'll show you how to use the Text Format toolbar to apply a style to a text block.

🎁 To apply a style to a text block:

1. If the Text Format toolbar is not in view, click **Open the Text Format Toolbar** **F** in the XML Editor's toolbar.

    > **Note** — You'll use the Styles list on the Text Format toolbar, not its formatting buttons.

    Suppose that you want to apply the h1 style to the following heading:

Tag bar —— **Growing grass**

Notice that the text block's tag bar shows h2. (The tag bar is labeled with the tag, which is named for the style that is applied to the text block.)

The style list on the Text Format toolbar also shows that h2 is currently applied.

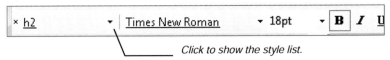

Click to show the style list.

2. Click anywhere in the text block where you want to apply a style.

3. From the style list on the Text Format toolbar, select the style you want to apply.

    The style you selected is applied to the text block and the text block's tag is changed to reflect the new style. (Notice in the example that the tag bar now shows h1.)

Applying a table style to a table

You apply a table style to a table when you add the table or by changing the table's properties later. Flare includes four factory table stylesheets.

🎁 To apply a table style to a table:

1. Either add the table as described on page 116 or change the table's properties by placing your cursor anywhere in the table and selecting **Table → Table Properties**. In either case, the Insert Table dialog opens (Figure 3-3 on page 112). In the Table Style section (Basic tab), notice that no table styles are listed.

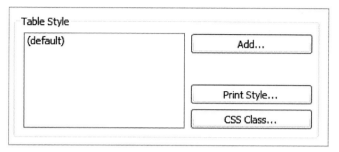

2. Click **Add**. The Select Table Style Template dialog opens.

3. To add one of the Flare templates, select **Factory Templates** in the Template Folders section. In the Templates section, select the table stylesheet you want to add, and click **OK**.

The stylesheet is added to the Table Style list on the Insert Table dialog and is automatically selected.

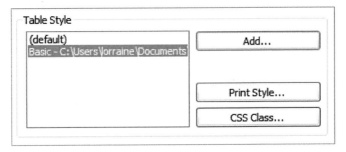

4. Click **OK.** The table in your topic is formatted with the
    characteristics of the table stylesheet that was selected in the
    Table Style section.

    Here is an example of a table formatted with the **Basic** table
    stylesheet.

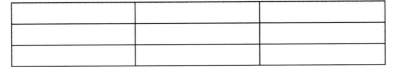

APPLYING A BACKGROUND COLOR TO YOUR TOPIC

 To apply a background color to a topic:

1. Select **Edit → Select All**.

2. Select **Format → Background Color**.

3. Pick the desired color from the color chart.

If you've applied a background color to text within the topic, its
background color will not change.

> ***Tip*** — To apply a background color to *all* topics in your project, change the
> background color for the body style in the Styles stylesheet. See "Editing styles"
> in the Flare Help system.

WHAT'S NEXT?

Now that you've formatted your content and added elements such as tables and images, it's time to think about how users will move around in your output.

Proceed to Step 4: Create Navigation Aids, to learn about the navigation aids—TOCs, links, bookmarks, cross-references, and indexes—that you can add to your project.

Step 4: Create Navigation Aids

STEP 5: Create Output
5A: Print Output
5B: Online Output

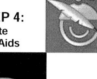

STEP 4:
Create
Nav Aids

STEP 3:
Develop
Content

STEP 2:
Learn the
XML Editor

STEP 1:
Get Started

In this chapter ...
➤ Create a TOC
➤ Create links
➤ Create bookmarks
➤ Test links
➤ Add cross-references
➤ Create index entries

OVERVIEW

This chapter discusses navigation aids that apply to both online and print output. To learn more about navigation aids that apply to online output only, see Step 5B: Create Online Output.

You can create these types of navigation aids with Flare:

- Table of Contents

- Links

- Cross-references

- Indexes

CREATING A TABLE OF CONTENTS

Flare's Table of Contents (TOC) feature is used for different purposes, depending on whether you're creating print or online output:

- **For online output,** users see the Flare TOC in the output. Users can use the TOC to browse for information and open things, such as topics, files, websites, or other linked items.

- **For print output,** users *do not* see the Flare TOC in the output. Users see only the Table of Contents that Flare built from the headings in topics. With print output, the Flare TOC is used as a topic outline when you build output.

With either output, you decide which topics to include.

A TOC gives your topics structure and can be used to organize content and to work in that structure. With Flare, you can create a TOC in two ways:

- By creating your topics and TOC simultaneously

- By creating your topics, creating your TOC, and linking TOC entries to your topics

Regardless of the method you choose, creating your project's TOC is your first step in building output.

Flare TOC files have an .fltoc file extension.

MULTIPLE *TOCs*

Flare allows you to create multiple TOCs. Why would you do this?

Suppose you need two TOCs for output that will contain different topics, such as "full" and "light" versions. Or perhaps you plan to build both print and online output, and you want your print output to include an index and a TOC.

Flare always labels one as the Master TOC.

MASTER *TOC*

When you create a new project, Flare creates a default TOC, which automatically becomes the Master TOC and is named "Master." You'll see it listed like this in the Project Organizer:

Figure 4-1:
Master
TOC

Designating a TOC as "master" allows you to take advantage of the toolbar button ⌗ Open Master TOC **Open Master TOC** and is useful for merging multiple TOCs into one. See "Linking TOCs" on page 147.

> **Best Practice** — Record the name of the Master TOC on the Target Settings form provided in Appendix A.

> **Note** — When you import a project, Flare creates a TOC that is named the same as the import file. This TOC is automatically designated as the Master TOC.

To designate a TOC as the master:

1. In the Project Organizer, expand the TOCs folder and right-click the TOC file you want to make into the master.

2. Select **Make Master TOC**.

WHAT CAN A *TOC* ITEM LINK TO?

A TOC item can link to any of the following:

- a topic in the current project

- an external file (a file outside of the project where the TOC resides)—even a PDF file!

- another TOC

- a website

- a browse sequence

- a target in another Flare project

- an external Help system

- a MadCap Mimic™ project or movie

LINKING TOCS

It's typical to link TOC items to topics in the same project, but you can link a TOC item to another TOC in order to merge the TOCs. For instance:

- If you share common content with other authors, you could create a TOC just for that content. Then you could share the TOC and its topics with the other authors.

- If multiple authors create topics that need to be merged for output, each author could create a TOC for their part of the output. A master TOC would link the TOCs to pull them together. (The TOCs would be merged when you build the output, and the result would be one seamless TOC.)

To see what a TOC item links to:

- Hover your cursor over the TOC item. You will see what the item links to in the Content Explorer.

CREATING A TOC

You can create a TOC before you begin creating topics or at any time thereafter. We find it easiest to create a TOC and add topics to your project simultaneously. However, if you prefer, you can add topics to your TOC later by simply dragging and dropping the topics from the Content Explorer.

To create a TOC:

1. In the Project Organizer, right-click the TOCs folder and select
    Add Table of Contents from the menu. The Add TOC dialog
    opens.

2. In the File Name field, type a name for the new TOC.

3. Click **Add**, then **OK** to add the new TOC.

    The new TOC is listed in the TOCs folder and opens in the TOC
    Editor.

To open a TOC:

-   In the Project Organizer, expand the TOCs folder and
    double-click the desired TOC.

    The TOC Editor opens in the middle pane and shows the
    contents of the TOC.

🔔 To add topics to a TOC:

- Drag and drop topics from the Content Explorer into the open TOC.

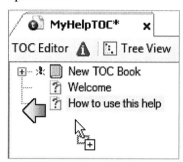

The text that appears in the TOC defaults to the topic's first heading.

OPENING A TOPIC OR THE PROPERTIES DIALOG

When you double-click a TOC item in a TOC, it will either open the topic in the XML Editor or open the Properties dialog for the topic. You control which action will occur with this button on the TOC Editor toolbar:

Toggle the double-click behavior: open topic or run properties dialog

This button acts as a toggle between the two modes.

> **Best Practice** — Set this button so that it opens a topic and leave it that way!

CREATING NEW BOOKS IN A TOC

TOC books allow you to create a hierarchy of topics in a TOC. Use them to organize your topics into a meaningful structure. TOC books can link to the same things that TOC items can, or they can link to nothing at all.

To create a new TOC book:

- Click **New book** in the TOC Editor toolbar.

Notice that the new TOC book isn't linked to anything yet.
When you create a new TOC book, Flare automatically creates a
new topic (called "New Entry") within it.

CREATING NEW TOC ITEMS

To create a new TOC item:

1. Select the TOC folder you want to add the item to.

2. Click **New item** in the TOC Editor toolbar.

New item

Create a new
topic and link
to it

Notice that the new TOC item isn't linked to anything yet. You can link a topic to a TOC item at any time by right-clicking and selecting **Link to Topic** from the menu.

> ***Note*** — To create a TOC item and topic simultaneously and link the two, click **Create a new topic and link to it** ⬚ instead of the **New item** ⬚ button.

RENAMING A TOC

 To rename a TOC:

1. In the Project Organizer, expand the TOCs folder.

2. Right-click the desired TOC and select **Rename** from the menu.

3. Type the new name and press **ENTER**.

REARRANGING ITEMS AND BOOKS IN A TOC

Use the following buttons on the TOC Editor toolbar to move TOC books and items left, right, up, or down in the TOC. Moving books and items to the left and right changes their hierarchy in the TOC.

⬅ ➡ ⬆ ⬇

CREATING LINKS

Flare lets you add various types of links to your topics.

TYPES OF LINKS

A link allows users to quickly jump to additional or related information. You can create links to:

- topics or files inside or outside your project

- information in the same topic

Links can be created for online and print output.

> **Note** — In Table 4-1, links in **boldface** are described in this book. Other types of links are described in Flare's Help system.

Table 4-1: Types of links

This link ...	Does this ...
Cross-reference	Jumps from text in one topic to another topic or bookmark within a topic. Can be used in online or print output, but are especially useful for print output. Unlike text hyperlinks, cross-references can include commands for inserting elements like page numbers and topic titles. The cross-reference link text is automatically updated by Flare when you build output. See ""Adding cross-references" on page 162 for more information.
Text hyperlink	Jumps to a specified location. See ""Creating text hyperlinks," next, for more information.
Text popup	Opens a popup that contains text you specify.
Topic popup	Opens a popup that contains another topic.
Bookmark	Jumps to a bookmark (a marker you create to identify a specific location in a topic). You can link to bookmarks in the same topic with a text hyperlink or in any topic with a cross-reference. See "Creating text hyperlinks," next, and "Creating bookmarks and linking to them" on page 159 for more information.
External link	Allows you to link to a file outside your project.
Image hyperlink	Opens a link associated with an image.

	This link ...	Does this ...
Table 4-1: *(Cont.)*	Movie link	Opens a link that plays a movie created with MadCap Mimic.
	Audio link	Opens a link that plays an audio file created with MadCap Echo™.
	Toggler	Hides and shows a piece of content. When a user clicks a "toggler hotspot," tagged content is shown or hidden (toggled).
	Drop-down text	Hides and shows a piece of content as a list. When a user clicks this type of link, content is displayed below the link.
	Expanding text	Hides and shows a portion of a paragraph. When a user clicks this type of link, the condensed paragraph is expanded for viewing.
	Concept link ("See Also" or "A-link")	Opens a group of topics related to the current topic.
	Related Topics link	Opens a topic related to the current topic. See "Creating related topics links" on page 158 for more information.
	Keyword link ("K-link")	Opens topics related to the current topic by using index keywords shared by both.
	Shortcut control	Launches an application program or window with a relationship to the current topic.

CREATING TEXT HYPERLINKS

A text hyperlink is a commonly used type of link that enables a user to jump to another location, such as:

- a heading or bookmark in the current topic

- a document that is currently open

- a topic in the same Content Explorer folder as the active topic

- a topic you have recently opened in your project

- any topic in the same project

- a topic outside your project

- a website

> **Note** — You can also set up an email address as a text hyperlink. When a user clicks the link, their email application opens with an email address in the "To" field.

We provide two ways to insert a text hyperlink. The first method is faster and links to another topic in the same project. The second method is used to link to anything else (listed above).

To insert a text hyperlink to a topic in the same project:

1. Open the topic in which to insert the link.

2. Make sure the Content Explorer is open.

3. In the topic, select the text you want to use as the link (the hotspot).

4. From the Content Explorer, drag and drop the topic onto the selected text. The Insert Hyperlink dialog opens.

5. Verify that **Topic in Project** is selected and click **OK**. The link is added to the topic. (By default, links appear as blue underlined text as shown below.)

Text hyperlink

Click here for more information about
website, you won't find information he
we hope to give you the help you need
inspire you to try new plants or design

To insert other types of text hyperlinks:

1. Open the topic in which you want to insert the link.

2. In the topic, select the text you want to use as the link (the hotspot). For this example, we selected "Growing grass."

3. Select **Insert → Hyperlink** or click **Insert a hyperlink** in the XML Editor toolbar. The Insert Hyperlink dialog opens.

4. Use the following chart to choose what you want to link to
    (listed in the Link to section of this dialog).

Use this option ...	To ...
Place in this Document	Link to headings or bookmarks in the topic. After selecting this option, use the right side of the dialog to select the place in the document to link to.
Document Currently Open	Link to another open topic in the project. After selecting this option, choose the document you want to link to or click **Bookmark** and select a location in the document.
File in Current Folder	Link to a topic in the same folder in the Content Explorer. After selecting this option, choose the file you want to link to or click **Bookmark** and select a location in the document.
Recent File	Link to a topic that was recently opened. After selecting this option, choose the document you want to link to or click **Bookmark** and select a location in the document.
Topic in Project	Link to a topic in the project. After selecting this option, click **Topic** to browse and open the topic you want to link to or click **Bookmark** and select a location in the document.
External Topic	Link to a topic or file (such as a PDF file) outside the project. After selecting this option, click **External Topic** to browse and open a topic you want to link to or click **Bookmark** and select a location in the document.
	After you choose an external topic, its path name appears to the right of the External Topic button.
	Important — To be sure that your output will link properly to the file, place a copy of the file in your project's Content folder before linking to it. Files located elsewhere (such as in the project folder) are not copied to the output folder.

Use this option ...	To ...
Website	Link to an external file, such as a website URL. After selecting this option, enter the complete URL (including the http://) in the Website field.
Email	Link to an email address. After selecting this option, enter the email address and subject in the appropriate fields or select a recent email address. For information about when this could be used, see Flare's Help system.

5. Use the following chart to choose optional link properties (listed in the Link Properties section of this dialog).

Use this option ...	To ...
Link text	Change the text that was selected as a link in the topic.
Target Frame	Select how the linked destination will open (such as in a new window).
Screen Tip	Specify text that appears when users hover the cursor over the link.
Style Class	Not covered in this book.

6. Click **OK**. The link is added to the topic. (By default, links appear as blue underlined text.)

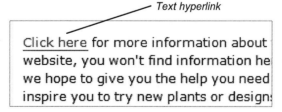

Text hyperlink

CREATING RELATED TOPICS LINKS

With related topics links, users can view information that is relevant to the current topic. Related topics links are used as "See also" would be used in a book index: to find additional information that you have decided pertains to the current topic.

To insert a related topics link:

1. Open the topic in which you want to insert the link.

2. Click in the topic where the link will be inserted (typically the bottom of the topic).

3. Select **Insert → Help Control → Related Topics Control**. The Insert Related Topics Control dialog opens.

4. In the Folders section, select the following to view topics:

Select ...	To view ...
(top)	Topics in the same folder as the current topic.
(all files)	All topics in the project.
a specific folder	Topics in the Content Explorer folder you chose.

The contents of the Files section changes, depending on what you select in the Folders section.

5. In the Files section, click a topic you want to add as a related topics link and click <<. The topic is added to the left side of the dialog. Repeat this step for each topic you want to add to the link.

6. Click **OK**. The link is added to the topic. (If Show Markers is turned on, related topics links appear as shown below.)

Selecting trees

Be sure to select plants that are suitable to your c(
buying trees and shrubs, consider these aspects of

- How much sunlight does the area get?
- Is the soil sandy? Is it mostly clay?
- How well does the soil drain?
- What is the PH of the soil?

Related topics link Do a soil test to answer these questions.

Related Topics

Best Practice — Apply an "online only" condition tag to the text block that contains the related topic link to prevent it from appearing as an extra line in print output. (When you build print output, Flare automatically removes Help control links from your topics, since they don't apply to print output. This could result in extra lines.)

CREATING BOOKMARKS AND LINKING TO THEM

Bookmarks allow you to place a marker in a topic so you can link to that text from within the topic or from another topic. First, you insert the bookmark, then you insert links to it.

To insert a bookmark:

1. Click in the topic where you want to insert the bookmark (typically at the beginning of a paragraph or heading).

2. Select **Insert → Bookmark**. The Manage Bookmarks dialog opens.

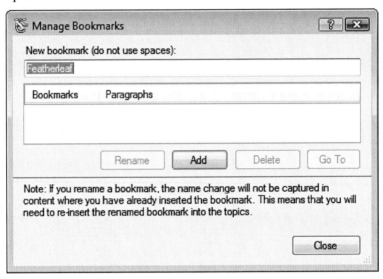

3. In the New bookmark field, type a bookmark name (without any spaces). If you clicked at the beginning of a text block, Flare places the first word in the New bookmark field.

4. Click **Add**. Flare marks the location with a bookmark icon and the bookmark name.

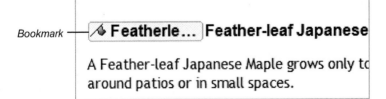

⚠ To insert a link to a bookmark in the same topic:

1. Select the text you want to link to.

2. Select **Insert → Hyperlink** or click **Insert a hyperlink** 🔗 in the XML Editor toolbar. The Insert Hyperlink dialog opens.

3. Select **Place in this Document**.

4. On the right side of the dialog, select the bookmark you want to link to.

5. Click **OK**. The link is added to the topic. (By default, links appear as blue underlined text.)

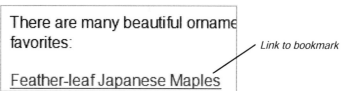

TESTING YOUR LINKS

You can test your links as you develop project content or test them all after you build your output. The choice is yours.

There are two ways to test your links. You can:

- Build your output, view it, and click on each link to be sure that it jumps to the proper location (topic, bookmark, URL, email address, etc.). Test your links in every topic.

- Preview a topic in the XML Editor and click on each link in that topic. See "Previewing a topic" on page 49.

ADDING CROSS-REFERENCES

Like a text hyperlink, a cross-reference lets a user jump to a topic or bookmark in a topic. But unlike text hyperlinks, cross-references have more formatting options and can include commands for inserting items such as page numbers and topic titles in the result.

ABOUT COMMANDS

Using commands allows Flare to automatically update cross-references when the destination's title, page number etc., change.

Let's see how commands work. Suppose you create a cross-reference to a topic that includes a title and page number:

> See "Adding an account" on page 23.

If you change the topic title to "Adding a user account" and build your output, Flare automatically updates the cross-reference with the new title:

> See "Adding a user account" on page 23.

> **Important** — If you change a topic's title, Flare updates cross-references to it. However, use caution when changing topic file names, or you could end up with errors (missing linked files) when you build the output.

CROSS-REFERENCES IN PRINT AND ONLINE OUTPUT

You can add cross-references to online output, but they are most useful for print output. By using stylesheet mediums, you can create one cross-reference format for online output (e.g., without page numbers) and another for print output (e.g., with page numbers).

When you create a new project, Flare creates three stylesheet mediums:

- Default

- Print

- Non-print

Cross-references use the MadCap:xref style. For the **default** and **non-print** mediums, the MadCap:xref style is set to:

> See "{paratext}"

For the **print** medium, the MadCap:xref style is set to:

> See "{paratext}" on page {page}

> *Note* — To use the cross-reference style defined by the print medium, select the print medium on the Advanced tab when you set up your target for print output. For more information about using mediums, see "What are mediums?" on page 86.

INSERTING A CROSS-REFERENCE

To insert a cross-reference:

1. Open the topic in which to insert the cross-reference.

2. In the XML Editor, place your cursor where you want to insert the cross-reference.

3. Select **Insert → Cross-Reference**. The Insert Cross-Reference dialog opens.

4.   Select what you want to link to by doing one of the following:

To link to ...	Do this ...
A heading or bookmark in the current topic	Select **Place in this document**. Then select the topic or bookmark you want to link to from the box on the right.
A topic that is currently open in the XML Editor	Select **Open document**. Then select the topic you want to link to from the box on the right. (To view and select a bookmark in the selected topic, click **Bookmark**.)
A topic in the same Content Explorer folder as the topic in which you are placing the cross-reference	Select **File in current folder**. Then select the topic you want to link to from the box on the right. (To view and select a bookmark in the selected topic, click **Bookmark**.)
A topic that you recently opened	Select **Recent file**. Then select the topic you want to link to from the box on the right. (To view and select a bookmark in the selected topic, click **Bookmark**.)

To link to ...	Do this ...
A topic in the open project	Select **Topic in Project**. Then click **Topic**, navigate to and select the topic file you want to link to, and click **Open**. (To view and select a bookmark in the selected topic, click **Bookmark**.)

This example shows the Insert Cross-Reference dialog after choosing a cross-reference to a topic in the open project.

Default cross-reference format

Preview of the cross-reference

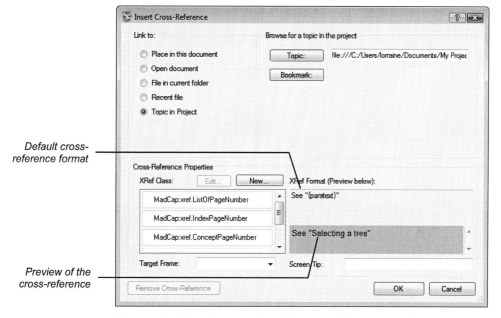

Notice the XRef Format (See "{paratext}") in the lower right part of the dialog. This is the format for the default medium.

> **Note** — The {paratext} command displays the *text* of the first *paragraph* (text block) in the linked topic. In the example above, "Selecting a tree" is the first text block. (It also happens to be the title of the topic.)

5. (*Optional*) From the Target Frame list, select an option (such as New Window) for opening the linked file. If you don't select an option, the topic opens in the same window as the topic that contains the cross-reference.

6. (*Optional*) In the Screen Tip field, type the phrase you want to appear when a user hovers the cursor over the cross-reference in the output.

7. Click **OK**. The cross-reference is added to the topic.

> For information about varieties of plants, See "Selecting a tree"

8. Click **Save All** ⬛ to save your work.

CHANGING CROSS-REFERENCES

You can change a cross-reference by:

- Changing the topic it links to

- Changing the target frame (how the linked topic opens in the output)

- Entering or changing the screen tip

- Changing the format of the cross-reference style, which changes the format for all cross-references that use that style.

> *Important* — The first three methods above change only a single cross-reference. The last one—changing the format of a cross-reference—affects *all* cross-references in your project that use that style.

Changing a single cross-reference

Use the following procedure to change the linked topic, target frame, or screen tip of a single cross-reference.

🎁 To change a single cross-reference:

1. Open the topic that contains the cross-reference you want to change.

2. Right-click the cross-reference and select **Edit Cross-Reference**. The Insert Cross-Reference dialog appears.

3. Change the cross-reference as described in Steps 4 – 8 of the procedure for inserting a cross-reference (page 163).

Changing the format of a cross-reference style

There are two ways to change the format of a cross-reference style. Both methods *change the style in your Styles stylesheet*. You can:

- Open a topic that contains a cross-reference that uses the style you want to change, and edit the style.

- Open the Stylesheet Editor and change the MadCap:xref style (or MadCap:xref.stylename, if you've created a class of the MadCap:xref style).

You'll learn the first method here. For more information about using the Stylesheet Editor, search on "Stylesheet Editor" in the Flare Help system.

To change the format of a cross-reference style:

1. Open any topic that contains a cross-reference with the style you want to change.

2. Right-click the cross-reference and select **Edit Cross-Reference**. The Insert Cross-Reference dialog appears.

3. In the Cross-Reference Properties section, select the <MadCap:xref> style you want to change.

   > *Note* — These instructions show you how to change the format of the MadCap:xref tag. If you create your own cross-reference style (a class of the MadCap:xref tag) and want to change it, select it instead.

4. Click **Edit**. The Edit Cross-Reference Style Class dialog opens.

5. In the Stylesheet to modify field, select the stylesheet you want to change.

> *Important* — These steps change the MadCap:xref style in the all three mediums (default, print, and non-print) for the stylesheet you select. (For more information about mediums, see "What are mediums?" on page 86.)

6. In the Enter format field, change the format as desired.

To insert ...	Do this ...
Text (e.g., "See" or "on page")	Type the text in the Enter format field.

To insert ...	Do this ...
A command	<ul><li>Click in the Enter format field where you want to insert the command.</li><li>Scroll in the command list and double-click the command you want to insert.</li></ul>

> *Note* — For commands such as adding boldface, you'll need to insert *both* a start and end tag into the Enter format field.

7. Click **OK**, then **Yes** to confirm that you want to redefine the existing style.

> *Note* — When you change a cross-reference style, you might not see the format change until you update the cross-reference.

UPDATING CROSS-REFERENCES MANUALLY

Updating cross-references manually is optional because Flare does this automatically when you build your output. However, you can update the appearance (format) and content of cross-references in the active topic at any time.

> *Tip* — When you change the format of a cross-reference, it's helpful to see what it looks like without building your output.

To update cross-references manually:

1. Open the topic that contains the cross-reference you want to update.

2. Select **Tools → Update Cross-References**. The Update Cross-References dialog appears, listing all cross-references in the active topic.

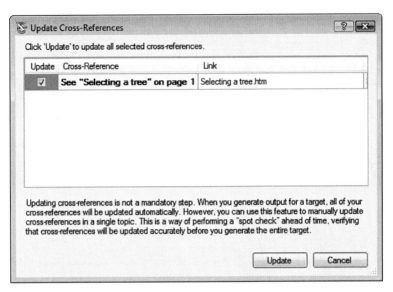

3. Click **Update**. The cross-references are updated in the active
    topic. Both the format and the content are updated.

ADVANCED FEATURES

You can do more with cross-references, such as:

▪   Creating context-sensitive cross-references in which the cross-
    reference link text reflects its proximity to the linked output if it
    appears on the same, previous, or next page.

▪   Using stylesheet mediums to format a cross-reference differently
    for print and online output. For example, a cross-reference can
    appear as "See 'Adding an account'" in your online output and
    "See 'Adding an account' on page 56" in your print output.

▪   Creating classes of the MadCap|xref style.

▪   Adding format commands.

These features are beyond the scope of this book. To learn more
about them, search on "cross-references" in the Flare Help system.

CREATING INDEX ENTRIES

Index entries are created in the same way, whether you're using them for print or online output. To create index terms, you must add index keywords to your topics before building your output. The keywords are added right in the topics.

> *Tip* — You can make index keywords conditional (by applying a condition tag) so that you can include only index terms applicable to the desired target. See the procedure called "To add multiple keywords, phrases, and multi-level keywords" that follows.

ADDING INDEX KEYWORDS

Here are two ways to add index keywords. The first method is fast, but it adds only a single-word index term—for the word your cursor is positioned on. The second method lets you add index keywords for phrases and multi-level indexes.

To add a single keyword:

1. Open the topic you want to insert index keywords into.

2. Click in the word (or immediately before or after it) you want to add a keyword for, and press **F10** or select **Tools → Index → Insert <word> as Indexed Keyword**.

    The word you clicked is added as an index keyword. If markers are visible, the marker appears where you clicked.

> *Tip* — To turn on markers, see "Viewing index keywords" on page 174.

Index keyword

Growing grass

Growing grass grass isn't very complicat about the conditions that grass needs to be

To add multiple keywords, phrases, and multi-level keywords:

1. Open the topic you want to insert index keywords into.

2. Click **Toggle Index Entry Mode** in the XML Editor's top toolbar to turn on Index Entry mode. The cursor changes to an index entry symbol, as shown here:

Feather-leaf Japanese Maple

*Index Entry
Mode cursor*

A Feather-leaf Japanese Maple grows only to suitable for planting around patios or in small

3. Click in the topic where you want to place an index entry.

4. Type the index keyword or phrase.

   The Index Entry window opens and shows your entry as you type it.

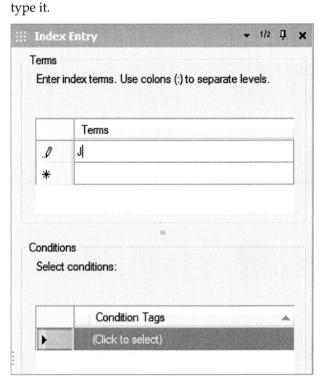

5. Press **ENTER**. The index entry is placed in your topic and the cursor moves to the next blank line in the Index Entry window. (If markers are turned on, you'll see the beginning of the entry where you placed it in the text.)

Index keyword (marker is turned on)

Feather-leaf Japanese Maple

A Feather-leaf Japanese Maple [Japanese M...] grows only to 6 feet tall, and is quite suitable for

6. To add more keywords to the same index marker, type a keyword on the next line and press **ENTER**. Continue adding index keywords to the same marker, as desired.

> **Note** — To create a multi-level index entry, separate the levels by a colon in the Index Entry window. In the example above, "trees:selecting" causes the term "selecting" to be listed under "trees" in the index.

Two-level index keyword

Feather-leaf Japanese Maple

[trees:select...] A Feather-leaf Japanese Maple [Japanese M...] grows only to 6 feet tall, and is quite suitable for planting around patios or in small spaces.

7. To apply a condition tag to the marker (to all of its keywords), click under the heading **Condition Tags** in the Conditions section of the Index Entry window. The Condition Tags dialog opens.

8. Check the condition tag (or tags) you want to apply to the index marker and click **OK**. The condition tag is applied to the marker and the color associated with that condition tag is shown on the marker in the topic.

Index marker with a condition tag applied

Feather-leaf Japanese Maple

trees:select... A Feather-leaf Japanese Maple ▉ Japanese M... grows only to 6 feet tall, and is quite suitable for planting around patios or in small spaces.

> *Note* — To learn more about condition tags, see "Using condition tags" on page 328.

9. When you're done adding entries to the index marker, click your cursor in a different spot in the topic to add another index marker.

10. When you're done adding index markers to the open topic, click **Toggle Index Entry Mode** again, then click anywhere in the topic. Now you'll be able to continue editing in the XML Editor.

Viewing index keywords

To see index keywords in a topic, you must have markers turned on.

To turn on markers:

- Click the arrow to the right of **Toggle show tags** in the XML Editor's top toolbar, and select **Show Markers**.

HOW INDEX ENTRIES APPEAR IN ONLINE OUTPUT

The index terms you add to your topics are shown in online output when you click the **Index** accordion bar. Index terms open the topics in which they were inserted. In the figures that follow, notice that "trees:selecting" was entered as the index keyword, which results in a two-level index entry for selecting trees.

Figure 4-2:
Index in online output

Index

Japanese Maple
perennials
   landscaping with
pruning trees
    equipment needed
    size considerations
trees
   selecting

📖 **TOC**

📄 **Index**

🔍 **Search**

HOW INDEX ENTRIES APPEAR IN PRINT OUTPUT

The index terms you add to your topics are shown in print output as a traditional index. Here's a print version of the index shown in Figure 4-2.

Figure 4-3:
Index in print output

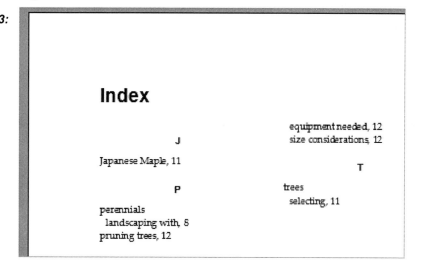

Index

J

Japanese Maple, 11

P

perennials
  landscaping with, 8
pruning trees, 12

equipment needed, 12
size considerations, 12

T

trees
  selecting, 11

CHANGING AND DELETING INDEX KEYWORDS

You can change the text of a marker's index keywords and remove keywords from a marker.

To change or remove a word from an index keyword:

1. Open the topic that contains the keyword you want to change or remove.

2. Make sure that markers are visible. If not, click the arrow to the right of **Toggle show tags** ⟨t⟩ ▾ in the XML Editor's top toolbar, and select **Show Markers**.

3. Right-click the marker to be changed and select **Edit Index Keyword** from the menu. The Index Entry window opens and shows the keywords contained in that marker.

4. Change or remove keywords as desired and press **ENTER**. Flare changes the marker's keywords. Close the Index Entry window if desired.

DELETING INDEX MARKERS

You can delete entire index markers, but **use caution** when doing so because this removes all keywords contained in that marker.

> **Note** — This procedure works for other kinds of markers too, not just index markers.

To delete an index marker:

1. Open the topic that contains the index marker you want to delete.

2. Make sure that markers are visible. If not, click the arrow to the right of **Toggle show tags** ⟨t⟩ ▾ in the XML Editor' top toolbar, and select **Show Markers**.

3. Right-click the marker to be deleted and select **Delete** from the menu. The marker is removed from the topic.

WHAT'S NEXT?

Now your online or print document is ready to be built into output. Refer to:

- Step 5A: Create Print Output (which includes PDFs)

- Step 5B: Create Online Output

You're almost there!

Step 5A: Create Print Output

STEP 5: Create Output
5A: Print Output
5B: Online Output

STEP 4:
Create
Nav Aids

STEP 3:
Develop
Content

STEP 2:
Learn the
XML Editor

STEP 1:
Get Started

In this chapter ...

- ➤ Learn about types of print output
- ➤ Create a simple print document
- ➤ Make upfront decisions
- ➤ Include front and back matter
- ➤ Discover page layouts
- ➤ Build your output

OVERVIEW

In this chapter, you'll learn how to build the following types of print output:

- Microsoft Word

- Adobe FrameMaker

- Adobe PDF

- Microsoft XPS

- XHTML

> ***Note*** — If you're unfamiliar with terms and concepts such as *output, build, distribute* and *target,* refer to the Document Basics chapter.

When you build print output, Flare puts the print output files in a folder in your project directory. You can then distribute those files to others. The type and number of files Flare creates depends on the type of print output you build.

KEEPING TRACK OF PRINT OUTPUT

To make it easier to track various targets and types of output, we've created a Target Settings form (see Appendix A). As you learn to create more targets for your output, you'll find it very helpful to record the names of various Flare project files.

We suggest that you keep a copy of this form handy as you proceed through this chapter and begin making it a habit to fill it out.

TYPES OF PRINT OUTPUT

This section describes the various types of print output, plus information about viewing and distributing your output.

MICROSOFT WORD OUTPUT

You can build Microsoft Word files that can be used with Microsoft Word 2003 and Microsoft Word 2007. The files can be created in one of these formats: DOC, XML, or DOCX (Word 2007 only).

By default, Flare creates a DOC file if you have MS Word 2003 and a DOCX file if you have MS Word 2007. Output is saved in a single file unless you set up the target to build multiple files. For more information, see the topic "Specifying Chapter Breaks and Page Layouts" in the Flare Help system.

> *Note* — If you want Flare to create a Word Table of Contents or an index, the content *must* be contained in a single file.

Distributing Word output

When you build your Word output, Flare does not embed images into the DOC, DOCX, or XML file. Instead, it stores the images in the Resources\Images folder (located in a sub-folder of the Output folder).

When you distribute your Word output, you must include the DOC, DOCX, or XML file *plus* the contents of the Resources folder, which contains ancillary files such as images.

> *Tip* — If you want to embed images into the document file so you can distribute it without the Resources folder, point your browser to the MadCap knowledge base (http://kb.madcapsoftware.com), search for "embedding images" and follow the instructions in "Article #: OUTPW1010F - Embedding Images in Word output."

ADOBE FRAMEMAKER OUTPUT

You can create FrameMaker documents for Adobe FrameMaker 7.0 and later versions in BOOK and FM formats. FrameMaker output is saved as multiple files, which consist of a BOOK file with associated FM files.

> *Tip* — If you want to save FrameMaker output in a single file, see the topic "Specifying Chapter Breaks and Page Layouts" in the Flare Help system.

Distributing FrameMaker output

When you distribute FrameMaker output, you must include the BOOK and FM files *plus* the contents of the Resources folder (located in a sub-folder of the Output folder). The Resources folder contains ancillary files, such as the images you've inserted into your topics.

ADOBE *PDF* OUTPUT

You can build PDF output by itself (available with Flare Version 4.0 and later) or with Microsoft Word or Adobe FrameMaker output. The output is saved in a single PDF file.

Distributing PDF output

The PDF file is the only file you need to distribute.

MICROSOFT *XPS* OUTPUT

XPS (XML Paper Specification) is a fixed layout, device-independent document format developed by Microsoft. You can build XPS output by itself or simultaneously with Microsoft 2007 output. XPS output is saved in a single XPS file.

> *Note* — This output format became available starting with Flare Version 4.0.

Table 5A-1:
Building
XPS
output

To build XPS output …	You must have …
By itself	Windows Vista
	- or -
	.NET Framework 3.0 installed on your computer (a free download from Microsoft).
Simultaneously with Microsoft 2007 output	Microsoft Word 2007
	– and –
	the "Save as XPS" add-in for Microsoft Office 2007 installed on your computer (a free download from Microsoft).

Viewing XPS output

You can view XPS output from within Flare or externally by opening the XPS output file.

Table 5A-2:
Viewing
XPS
output

To view XPS output ...	You must have ...
From within Flare (immediately after building the output)	Internet Explorer 7 or higher. Flare uses MadCap's built-in Book Viewer, which opens Internet Explorer or lets you browse for it (if it's not your default browser).
Outside of Flare on a computer running Vista	Internet Explorer 7 or higher.
Outside of Flare on a computer running XP	.NET Framework 3.0 installed on your computer – and – Internet Explorer 7 or higher. Both are free downloads from Microsoft.

Distributing XPS output

The XPS file is the only file you need to distribute.

XHTML OUTPUT

XHTML is a browser-based XML document format. You can view an XHTML document online or print it. Regardless of the number of topics, XHTML output is saved in a single file with an .htm extension.

> ***Note*** — This output format became available starting with Flare Version 4.0.

Distributing XHTML output

When you distribute your output, you must include the HTM file *plus* the contents of the Resources folder. The Resources folder contains ancillary files, such as the images you've inserted into your topics.

BEFORE CREATING PRINT OUTPUT

Before you create print output, you should do the following:

- **Create your project**. You can build print output from any Flare project. To create the project, see "Creating a Flare project" on page 39.

- **Create and format your content**. You create and format content for print output as you would for any other output as described in Step 2: Learn the XML Editor, and Step 3: Develop Content.

- **Add navigation aids**. Use Step 4: Create Navigation Aids, to add cross-references, links, and index entries.

- **Verify that you have a target for the type of print output you want to create**. If not, add the target. See "Adding a target" on page 57.

WHAT YOU CAN INCLUDE IN A PRINT DOCUMENT

Your print output can contain any of the following front and back matter parts, which you'll learn more about later in this chapter:

- Table or Contents
- index
- glossary
- endnotes
- list of elements
- list of concepts

MAKE DECISIONS

It's time for some decisions!

DECISION TIME!

Before you continue, you need to think about the document parts your output needs to contain, how it should be oriented, and its size.

Do you need these front or back document parts?

- ✓ Title page
- ✓ Table of Contents
- ✓ List of elements
- ✓ List of concepts
- ✓ Endnotes
- ✓ Glossary
- ✓ Index

How should the print output be oriented?

- ✓ Portrait
- ✓ Landscape
- ✓ A combination of both

What size does your document need to be?

- ✓ Letter
- ✓ Legal
- ✓ A4
- ✓ Custom size

Appendix A contains detailed planning worksheets to help you record your decisions.

OUR RECOMMENDATION

In this chapter, you'll learn how to create both a simple print document and a more complex one—one with multiple document parts. For the more complex document, we've provided a tutorial.

We think it's best to climb the learning curve one step at a time. Therefore, we suggest that you create a simple print document as described next before attempting to create a document with front and back matter.

If all you need is a simple print document, read only the next section. Otherwise, take a look at "Creating a more complex print document" starting on page 188.

CREATING A SIMPLE PRINT DOCUMENT

If you need to create only a simple print document (no title page, TOC, index, or glossary), read this section. This is the quickest way to produce print output because it requires the least amount of setup.

To create a simple print document, you'll do the following:

- Create a topic outline (a Flare TOC), which tells Flare which topics to print and in what order.

- Edit the target for the type of print output you want.

- Build the output.

Use the following procedure to create a simple print document (one that uses the same page layout throughout) in a format that Flare supports (Word, FrameMaker, PDF, XPS, or XHTML).

 To create a simple print document:

1. Create a TOC that includes the topics to be printed in the desired print order. See "Creating a Table of Contents" on page 144. Flare uses this TOC as an outline when building the output.

   > ***Note*** — Your TOC can be as simple as a list of topics if that's all you need.

2. In the Project Organizer, expand **Targets** and double-click the desired target. The Flare Target Editor opens to the last open tab.

3. Click the **Basic** tab if not already open.

4. Select the Output Type. Use the following chart as a guide.

Select ...	To produce this type of output ...
FrameMaker	Adobe FrameMaker document alone
	Adobe FrameMaker and PDF documents simultaneously
PDF	PDF
Word	Microsoft Word document alone
	Microsoft Word and PDF documents simultaneously
	Microsoft Word and XPS documents simultaneously
XHTML Book	XHTML document alone
XPS	XPS

> **Note** — To build XPS output alone, you must have Microsoft.NET Framework 3.0 installed on your computer. If you don't, a free download is available at www.microsoft.com.

5. In the Master TOC field, select the TOC to use as an outline (if not already selected).

6. (*Optional*) If you want to produce two types of output simultaneously (such as Word and PDF), click the **Printed Output** tab. In the FrameMaker and MS Word Output section, check the desired options.

```
┌─ FrameMaker and MS Word Output ──────────────────────────────┐
│                                                              │
│   ☐  Generate PDF for FrameMaker and MS Word Output   (quick help) │
│                                                              │
│   ☐  Generate XPS for MS Word Output   (quick help)          │
│                                                              │
│   ☐  Generate multiple documents for MS Word output   (quick help) │
│                                                              │
│   ☐  Generate "Mirror Margins" for MS Word Output   (quick help) │
│                                                              │
│   ☐  Disable Master Pages for FrameMaker and MS Word output   (quick help) │
│                                                              │
└──────────────────────────────────────────────────────────────┘
```

> ***Note*** — If you're setting up a FrameMaker target, only the first and last checkboxes are available.

7. Click **Save All** 🖫 to save your selections plus any other project files (such as the TOC) that you created.

8. In the Project Organizer under **Targets**, right-click the target you just set up and select **Build <target name>** from the menu.

   Flare builds the output according to the selections you made. If your project is large, this might take several seconds.

9. View the output when prompted or view it later.

   When you're ready to distribute your output, you'll find it in a folder under your project's Output folder. The file is in a folder named for the target used to build output.

Now that you've created a simple print document, let's get more ambitious!

CREATING A MORE COMPLEX PRINT DOCUMENT

We've developed a tutorial to show you how to create a document that's more complex—one with front and back parts.

Keep in mind that there are many ways to accomplish the same result. How you set up print output depends in part on how you arrange content in your Flare topic files. For instance, one person might put a document's title and copyright text into a single topic and another might put them into two separate topics.

In this tutorial, you'll learn one way of setting up a more complex document.

HOW TO USE THIS TUTORIAL

There's a lot to learn here. Because it's so easy to focus intently on the detailed instructions of a tutorial, you can miss the significance of what you're doing. We suggest that you go through this tutorial a few times. The real learning happens after you step back from the details and can see the big picture.

So, let's get to it!

This tutorial teaches you how to create a PDF document that contains a title, copyright text, Table of Contents, two chapters, and an index. We suggest that you **set aside at least two hours** to complete this entire tutorial.

SAMPLE DOCUMENT

Our sample output will have these characteristics:

- portrait orientation

- page size of 8.5 x 11 inches

- page margins of one inch on three sides (top, bottom, outside) and 1.5 inches on the inside. (The Flare page-layout templates you're going to use for this tutorial have a 1.5 inch inside margin.)

- two-column index

- chapters starting on an odd page

- chapters ending on an even page (whether the page has content or not)

The following illustrations show what you'll be creating in the tutorial.

Figure 5A-1:
Title page

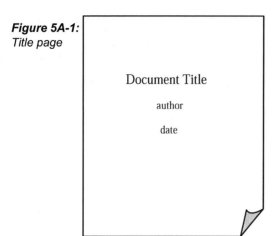

Specs: *First page in the document starts on the right; no header, footer or page number.*

Figure 5A-2:
Copyright page

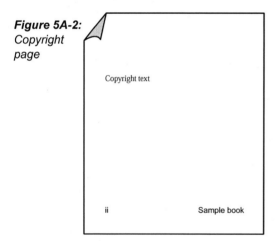

Specs: *Second page in the document starts on the left; no header. Footer contains the words "Sample book." Roman numeral page number.*

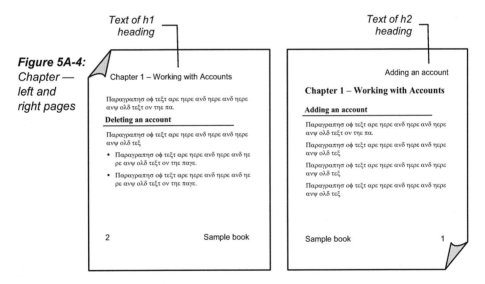

Figure 5A-3:
Table of
Contents —
left and
right pages

Contents

iv   Sample book

Contents

Sample book   v

Specs: Header contains the word "Contents." Footer contains the words "Sample book." Roman numeral page numbers.

Text of h1
heading

Text of h2
heading

Figure 5A-4:
Chapter —
left and
right pages

Chapter 1 – Working with Accounts

Παραγραπησ οφ τεξτ αρε ηερε ανδ ηερε ανδ ηερε ανψ ολδ τεξτ ον τηε πα.

Deleting an account

Παραγραπησ οφ τεξτ αρε ηερε ανδ ηερε ανδ ηερε ανψ ολδ τεξ

- Παραγραπησ οφ τεξτ αρε ηερε ανδ ηερε ανδ ηε ρε ανψ ολδ τεξτ ον τηε παγε.
- Παραγραπησ οφ τεξτ αρε ηερε ανδ ηερε ανδ ηε ρε ανψ ολδ τεξτ ον τηε παγε.

2   Sample book

Adding an account

Chapter 1 – Working with Accounts

Adding an account

Παραγραπησ οφ τεξτ αρε ηερε ανδ ηερε ανδ ηερε ανψ ολδ τεξτ ον τηε πα.

Παραγραπησ οφ τεξτ αρε ηερε ανδ ηερε ανδ ηερε ανψ ολδ τεξ

Παραγραπησ οφ τεξτ αρε ηερε ανδ ηερε ανδ ηερε ανψ ολδ τεξ

Παραγραπησ οφ τεξτ αρε ηερε ανδ ηερε ανδ ηερε ανψ ολδ τεξ

Sample book   1

Specs: Header text uses h1 style (left page) and h2 style (right page). Footer contains the words "Sample book." Decimal (1, 2, 3) page numbers.

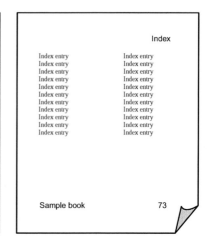

Figure 5A-5:
Index —
left and
right pages

Specs: Header contains the word "Index." Footer contains the words "Sample book." Decimal (1, 2, 3) page numbers.

Complete all of the tasks in this tutorial to learn how to set up and build a more complex document with front and back matter. Read on to learn about the tasks you're going to complete.

TUTORIAL TASKS

- **Task 1**: Create a topic for each front and back matter part to be included in the output (e.g., Table of Contents, glossary, index). These topics are placeholders for content.

- **Task 2**: Create a topic outline (Flare TOC), which tells Flare which topics to print and in what order.

- **Task 3**: Add a page layout for each document part.

- **Task 4**: Delete unneeded pages from page layouts.

- **Task 5**: Customize footers.

- **Task 6**: Customize headers.

- **Task 7**: Link page layouts to topics in the Flare TOC.

- **Task 8**: Set up the print target.

- **Task 9**: Build the print output.

Tutorial setup

Before you begin this tutorial, make sure you have completed these setup tasks:

- Create a project. (See "Creating a Flare project" on page 39.) Select **MyPDF** for the target.

- Add topics with these names (See "Adding a topic" on page 45):
    - **Title**
    - **Chapter 1**
    - **Overview**
    - **Starting your application**
    - **Chapter 2**
    - **Adding accounts**

Task 1: Create placeholder topics

In this tutorial, you'll create two special topics:

- Table of Contents

- Index

These topics are different from regular Flare topics because you don't type content (other than a topic heading) into them. Instead, Flare inserts a placeholder, called a **proxy**, into the topic.

When you build your output, the proxy is automatically replaced with the actual content. Flare builds the print Table of Contents from your headings and the index from index markers you'll place in your topics.

> *Note* — You don't need to do anything special with the title/copyright topic and chapter topics. They're just normal Flare topics into which you would type content.

You'll start by creating a topic for the TOC proxy.

1. Select **Project → Add Topic**. On the Add New Topic dialog, do the following:

    a. *If using Flare Version 4.2 and late*r, select **Factory Templates** for the folder, select **TopicForTOC.htm** for the template, and skip Steps 3 and 4 of this procedure.

    b. Type **Print TOC** for the File name.

    c. Type **Contents** for the 1st Heading.

    d. Click **Add**, then **OK** to copy the file to your project.

    The new topic is copied to the Content Explorer.

    > ***Best Practice*** — It's helpful to give the TOC a meaningful file name such as **<your project name> Print TOC** to distinguish it from any other TOCs you might have in your project.
    >
    > This is also a good example of a case in which you might *type* the 1st heading instead of leaving it blank. If you leave it blank, Flare uses the File name for the 1st heading.

    When you build your output, Flare builds the print Table of Contents from heading styles in your topics.

    > ***Tip*** — To prevent the h1 heading in the Table of Contents topic from being listed in the print Table of Contents, use a style other than h1 – h6 for the heading. For example, you might use the "p" paragraph style and apply local formatting to make it look like the h1 style.

2. With the new topic (Print TOC) open, delete the following text, (which came from the Flare template prior to Version 4.2):

    Delete this text and replace it with your own content.

    > ***Note*** — If you're using Flare Version 4.2 or later, delete the text from the template (except for the heading).

3. *If using Flare Version 4.1 and earlier,* select **Insert → Proxy → Insert TOC Proxy**. The TOC Proxy dialog opens.

Note — It is not necessary to select a stylesheet class (style) because Flare uses a default class for your TOC. In fact, you won't see any classes listed here unless you already created stylesheet classes (an advanced feature not included in this book).

4. *If using Flare Version 4.1 and earlier,* click **OK**.

The Table of Contents will go here when you build your output.

The placeholder topic is created and the output toc proxy appears in the topic.

5. Click **Save All** to save your work.

Now you'll create a topic to hold the index.

6. Select **Project → Add Topic**. On the Add New Topic dialog, do the following:

   a. *If using Flare Version 4.2 and later*, select **Factory Templates** for the folder, select **TopicForIndex.htm** for the template, and skip Steps 8 and 9 of this procedure.

   b. Type **Print Index** for the File name.

   c. Type **Index** for the 1st Heading.

   d. Click **Add**, then **OK** to copy the file to your project.

   The new topic is copied to the Content Explorer.

7. With the new topic (Print Index) open, delete the following text, (which came from the Flare template prior to Version 4.2):

   Delete this text and replace it with your own content.

   > ***Note*** — If you're using Flare Version 4.2 or later, delete the text from the template (except for the heading).

8. *If using Flare Version 4.1 and earlier*, select **Insert → Proxy → Insert Index Proxy**. The Index Proxy dialog opens.

9. *If using Flare Version 4.1 and earlier*, click **OK** to accept the defaults on this dialog.

The index will go here when you build your output.

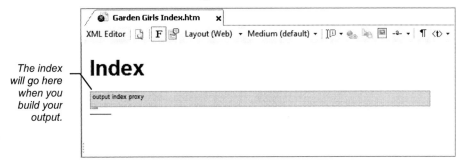

The placeholder topic is created and the output index proxy appears in the topic.

10. Click **Save All** 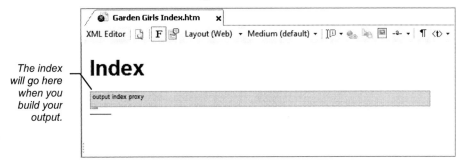 to save your work.

Creating the topic for the index isn't the only thing you need to do to create an index. You also need to add index keywords, which are used to create the index entries. (To create index keywords, see "Creating index entries" on page 171.)

TASK 2: CREATE A TOPIC OUTLINE

In this task, you'll create a topic outline that contains all of the topics you want to include in your output.

Using Flare's TOC feature, you'll add the regular topics (Title Page, Chapter 1, Overview, Starting your application, Chapter 2, and Adding accounts) plus entries for the Table of Contents and index topics you just created.

> *Important* — The text in the TOC you are creating as a topic outline does *not* become the Table of Contents in your print output. *Flare uses it only to locate the topics to include and build them in the proper order.*

Now you'll create the topic outline for your print (PDF) output.

1. In the Project Organizer, expand the TOCs folder and double-click **Master (Master)**. The TOC Editor opens with the beginnings of a TOC, which includes a starter topic called "Topic."

2. In the Master TOC, right-click **Topic** and select **Delete** from the menu.

3. Click **Save All** to save your changes.

   So now you have an empty TOC, and you're ready to build your topic outline.

4. Open the Content Explorer to view the list of topics in your project. You should have the eight topics you created (Chapter 1.htm, Chapter 2.htm, Overview.htm, Starting your application.htm, Adding accounts.htm, Print Index.htm, Print TOC.htm, and Title.htm) plus the starter topic (Topic.htm) that Flare added when you created your project.

   Let's get rid of the starter topic.

5. In the Content Explorer, right-click **Topic.htm** and select **Delete** from the menu. Click **OK** in response to the confirmation message. (If the Link Update dialog appears, click **Remove Links**.)

   Now you'll add your topics to the TOC in the order you want them to appear in your print output.

6. Drag **Title.htm** to the TOC Editor. Next, drag each topic to the TOC Editor and drop them in the order shown here:

   Print TOC
   Chapter 1
   Overview
   Starting your application
   Chapter 2
   Adding accounts
   Print Index

Your Master TOC should now look like this.

If it doesn't match, use the "Move item ..." buttons

in the TOC Editor's toolbar to place all topics
the same level.

Now you'll learn how to change the hierarchy of topics in
the TOC.

7. In the TOC Editor, select the topic called **Overview** and click

    Move item to the right in the TOC Editor toolbar. Notice
    that the Chapter 1 topic becomes a book when Overview is
    nested beneath it.

    Next move the topics **Starting your application** and **Adding
    accounts** to the right using the same method.

Your TOC Editor window should now look like this:

Content Explorer ▾ 1/2 ⊿ ✕	Outline for PDF output ✕
	TOC Editor ⚠ Tree View ▾
☐ Content	Title
⊞ Resources	Contents
Adding accounts.htm	Chapter 1
Chapter 1.htm	Overview
Chapter 2.htm	Starting your application
Overview.htm	Chapter 2
Print Index.htm	Adding accounts
Print TOC.htm	Index
Starting your application.htm	
Title.htm	

The TOC shows the Topic Title (Index), not its file name (Print Index.htm).

The order in which the topics are arranged in the TOC Editor dictates their order in the output.

Next, you'll rename the TOC. This next step isn't necessary, but it will help you keep things straight as your project grows.

8. In the Project Organizer, expand the **TOCs** folder (if necessary), right-click **Master (Master)** and select **Rename** from the menu. Then type **Outline for PDF output** and press **ENTER**. (You can also do this from Windows Explorer if you'd like.)

The "Master" is your main TOC.

TOC name

9. Click **Save All** to save your work.

Let's close all open documents before moving on to Task 3.

10. Select **Window → Close All Documents**. The middle pane is now empty.

> **Note** — To create multiple output documents with different topic outlines, create one TOC for each topic outline.

Next you'll specify **page layouts**, which are files that store your layout choices.

TASK 3: ADD PAGE LAYOUTS

You'll create a page layout from a page layout template provided by Flare, starting with the Title page.

1. Select **Project → Add Page Layout**. The Add New Page Layout dialog opens.

2. Make sure that **Factory Templates** is selected for the folder.

3. In the Templates section, select the **FrontMatterResizable.flpgl** template. (See page 221 for a description of each template.)

> **Note** — The template you're selecting is a page-layout template. Don't confuse this with a topic template.

4. Type **Title Pg Layout** in the File name field.

5. Click **Add**, then **OK** to copy the new page layout.

The file is copied to your project's Resources folder and appears under "PageLayouts" in the Content Explorer. (You can ignore the default page layout if you see one listed. You won't use it in this tutorial. Flare places it there when you create a new project.)

The page layout you created opens in the Page Layout Editor.

Now you need to create three more page layouts—one for the TOC, one for chapters, and one for the index.

6. Repeat Steps 1 – 5 in this procedure three times, using this chart as a guide. On the Add New Page Layout dialog:

Select this template ...	Type this for the File name ...
FrontMatterResizable.flpgl	TOC Pg Layout
ChapterResizable.flpgl	Chapter Pg Layout
IndexResizable.flpgl	Index Pg Layout

When you're done, your four page layouts are listed in the Content Explorer, as shown here:

Each page layout should be open in the Page Layout Editor (as indicated by the tabs at the top of the Page Layout Editor).

TASK 4: DELETE PAGES FROM PAGE LAYOUTS

Page layout templates provide a starting point only. You'll probably need to customize the page layouts the first time you create print output. After that, you can reuse them each time you print the same output.

> *Tip* — You can also copy page layouts, so that once you set up the layouts for one output document, you can replicate the layouts for others.

Page layouts can contain up to six page types: First, Title, Left, Right, Normal, and Empty. (See page 222 for more information about page types.) You won't need some of the pages on some of the layouts.

You'll work in the Page Layout Editor to customize the page layouts you just created. First, you'll remove the pages you don't need.

> *Best Practice* — Remove the pages that you don't need to keep your page layouts tidy and eliminate uncertainty about which pages you're using.

1. If you don't see all four tabs in the middle pane, click to the right of the Page Layout Editor tabs to view a list of the open page layouts.

2. Select **Title Pg Layout.flpgl** from the list (or by clicking its tab).

3. At the right side of the Page Layout Editor, right-click the Title page and select **Remove Page**.

> **Note** — To store the title page text and the copyright text in different topics, create a layout that has T (title) and E (empty) pages only (as discussed in the Flare Help system). However, if you want to combine the title page text and the copyright text into one physical topic file, we suggest that you use the F (first) page for the title and the L (left) page for the copyright page as we've done in this tutorial. Otherwise, you may get unexpected results.

4. Remove the page labeled **R** (right) and the page labeled **E** (empty).

    What remains is the **F** (first) page and the **L** (left) page, which you'll use for the copyright text.

5. Remove these pages from these page layouts:

From this page layout ...	Remove these pages ...
TOC Pg Layout.flpgl	(F) and (T)
Chapter Pg Layout.flpgl	(F)
Index Pg Layout.flpgl	(F)

Notice that you didn't delete the **E** (empty) pages for these layouts. That's because we want Flare to start each part (chapter, index, etc.) on an odd (right) page. If your layout includes the **Empty** page, Flare will pad the end of the previous chapter with an empty page if necessary in order to begin this chapter on an odd page.

6. Click **Save All** to save your work.

There are two more tasks for you to do to finish setting up the page layouts—customizing the header and footer frames.

TASK 5: CUSTOMIZE FOOTERS

You'll continue working with the Page Layout Editor to customize the footer frames of the page layouts you just created.

Let's start with the chapter page layout (see Figure 5A-4 on page 191). Once you've set up the left and right footers, you'll copy them to the other layouts to save yourself some time.

For this tutorial, this is what you want the left footer to look like.

1	Sample book

1. Click the **Chapter Pg Layout.flpgl** Page Layout Editor tab and complete the following tasks:

    a. Click the **Left** page. Scroll down to the footer frame and select it.

    footer · 'F2' to edit text

    The footer frame contains a centered page number, which is not what you want for this tutorial, so you need to edit it.

    b. Press **F2** to open the Frame Contents window.

You'll use the Frame Contents window to add and change content in page layout frames. It contains some of the XML Editor tools just for this purpose. Notice that the frame contains the variable "PageNum" (but not in a two-column table), so you'll delete it.

c. In the Frame Contents window, triple-click the text block to select the PageNum variable and the dashes that surround it. Then press **Delete**.

Flare normally aligns all of the text within a footer as either left, right, centered, or justified. However, this tutorial example is more complex (but also quite typical). We want the page number left aligned and the words "Sample book" right aligned. How can you do this? With a two-column table in the footer!

d. Select **Table → Insert → Table**, and set these properties on the Basic tab of the Insert Table dialog:

Set this property ...	To ...
Number of columns	2
Number of rows	1
Number of header rows	0
Number of footer rows	0
AutoFit Behavior	Fixed column width

Set this property ...	To ...
Fixed column width	3.00 in

> **Note** — Here's how we calculated 3 inches for the column width:
>
> | | 8.5 inches | (page size) |
> |---|---|---|
> | − | 1.0 inch | (right margin) |
> | − | 1.5 inch | (left margin) |
> | = | 6.0 inches | (space for text) |
>
> Divided by 2 columns = 3 inches per column

e.   Click **OK**.

Now you'll insert the page number variable into the table.

f.   Click inside the left cell of the table and select **Insert** → **Variable**. The Variables dialog opens.

g.   Select **System** for the Variable Set and **PageNumber** for the variable name, then click **OK**. The page number variable is shown in the cell of the table.

Don't worry about the format or starting page number for now. You'll set these in Task 7 when you link your page layouts to topics in the topic outline.

h.   Click inside the right cell of the table and type **Sample book**. Then click **Align Right** on the Text Format toolbar. (If not in view, open the toolbar by clicking **Open the Text Format Toolbar** **F**.) Your footer should now look like this:

| PageNum... 1 | Sample book |

i.   Save the footer by clicking **Save File** in the Frame Contents window, then close the Frame Contents window by clicking its close button (**x**).

Leave the Chapter Pg Layout's Left footer frame in view. You're going to use it again.

2.   Since all left pages of this tutorial use this same footer, you'll copy and paste the footer you just created to other left pages. Copying is faster than recreating the footer everywhere you need it.

To copy the footer:

a.   On the **Chapter Pg Layout Left** page, select the footer frame and press **CTRL + C** to copy it.

b.   Click the **Title Pg Layout.flpgl** tab, click the Left page, scroll down and select the footer frame, then press **Delete**. Now press **CTRL + V** to paste the frame you just copied.

c.   Click **Save All** and close the Title Pg Layout. You're done setting it up.

d. Paste the Chapter Pg Layout Left-page footer frame to these layouts in the same manner. (Don't forget to delete the frame you don't want before pasting the new one.)

In this page layout ...	Paste into these pages ...
Chapter Pg Layout	Empty page
TOC Pg Layout	Left page and Empty page
Index Pg Layout	Left page and Empty page

3. Next you're going to create the right page footer by copying the left page footer and swapping the contents of the table cells.

This is what you want the footer to look like.

Sample book	1

Complete the following tasks:

a. Click the **Chapter Pg Layout** tab and copy its Left page footer frame. Select the **Right** page and delete its footer. Paste the Left page footer frame into the Right page. Select the footer frame and press **F2.** Switch the contents of the cells so the words "**Sample book**" are in the left table cell and the page number is in the right table cell. Don't forget to save the changes in the Frame Contents window.

b. Copy and paste the right footer frame into the **Right** pages of the **TOC Pg Layout** and the **Index Pg Layout**.

4. Click **Save All** to save your work.

Now that both the left and right footers are set up for all pages in your page layouts, you'll set up the header frames.

TASK 6: CUSTOMIZE HEADERS

Both the Table of Contents and Index have headers that contain text you type (no variables). We'll set up the Table of Contents header first. We want the word "Contents" to appear on both left and right pages.

1. Click the **TOC Pg Layout.flpgl** tab and complete the following tasks:

    a. Click the Left page, scroll up and select the header frame, and press **F2**.

    b. In the Frame Contents window, type **Contents**. Then save your work by clicking **Save File** in the Frame Contents window, and close the Frame Contents window by clicking its close button (**x**).

    c. Copy the Left page header frame you just created, and paste it into the Empty page. (This way, if Flare needs to pad the end of a chapter with an empty page, the page will have a header.)

    d. Click the Right page, select the header frame, and press **F2**.

    e. In the Frame Contents window, type **Contents**. Then save your work (**Save File**) and close the Frame Contents window.

    f. Close the **TOC Pg Layout**. You're done setting it up.

    Next, you'll set up the header for the Index.

2. Click the **Index Pg Layout.flpgl** Page Layout Editor tab and complete the following tasks:

    a. Click the Left page, scroll up and select the header, and press **F2**.

First index term on the page

Index: [·FirstIndexTerm: ·] — [·LastIndexTerm: ·]

Last index term on the page

Notice the variables for first and last index term. (These variables came from the index template.) Although these variables can be used when creating PDF output, you're not using them for this tutorial, so you'll delete them.

b. In the Frame Contents window, select the text block (triple-click or use any other method for selecting the entire block) then press **Delete**.

c. Type **Index**. Then save the frame and close the Frame Contents window.

d. Copy the **Left** page frame you just saved and paste it into the Empty page.

e. Click the **Right** page, select the header, and press **F2**. Delete the first and last index term variables as you did for the Left page header. Type **Index**. Then save the frame (**Save File**) and close the Frame Contents window.

f. Close the **Index Pg Layout**. You're done setting it up.

One more layout to finish—the Chapter Pg Layout.

The Chapter Pg Layout needs headers that show the text of the h1 heading on the left pages and the text of the h2 heading on the right pages. You'll see how to set that up now.

3. Click the tab for **Chapter Pg Layout.flpgl** and complete the following tasks:

a. Click the **Right** page, scroll up and notice what's in the header frame.

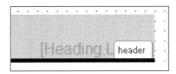

Although it's partially covered, the right page header frame contains the variable Heading.Level1, which places the text of the first h1 heading on the page in your running header when you build your output. We'll delete this and insert Heading.Level 2 (the variable for the h2 heading).

b. Select the header frame, press **F2**, right-click the variable, and select **Delete** from the menu. Now select **Insert →
Variable**.

c. From the Variables dialog, select **Heading** for the Variable Set and **Level 2** for the Name, and click **OK**. Then save the frame and close the Frame Contents window.

d. Now click the **Left** page, scroll to the left and look at the header frame.

The ChapterResizable template contains a variable that places a "Chapter" number in the left page header. What Flare calls a chapter is not necessarily what you might call a chapter.

Flare's "chapter number" represents the order of the topic files in your topic outline. In our example, Flare would consider our Title page topic to be "Chapter 1" and our Table of Contents to be "Chapter 2." It would consider our real Chapter 1 to be "Chapter 3."

For some documents, this would work just fine. But for our sample, this doesn't accurately represent our document's structure.

For our Chapter 1, we want the text of the first heading in the chapter to appear in the header of left pages. You'll insert the Level 1 variable to do this.

e. Select the header frame, press **F2**, triple-click to select all, then press **Delete**.

  f. Select **Insert → Variable**.

  g. From the Variables dialog, select **Heading** for the Variable Set and **Level 1** for the Name, then click **OK**. Save the frame (**Save File**) and close the Frame Contents window.

  Notice that Heading.Level 1 now appears in the header frame.

  h. Select the header frame you just set up and copy it. Click the Empty page and paste the frame into it.

4. Click **Save All** and close the Chapter Page Layout.

Whew! You're done setting up page layouts. It seems like a lot of work, but once you get comfortable with using Flare's page layout features, you'll likely find that shortcuts (such as copying and pasting frames) make setup quicker. Plus, once your page layouts are set up the way you want them, you won't have to do it again unless you want to change them.

> *Tip* — If you have other documents that use the same layout, you can copy your layouts to the Content\Resources\PageLayout folder of another Flare project.

TASK 7: LINK PAGE LAYOUTS TO TOPICS IN THE TOC

After getting the page layouts the way you want them, you'll tell Flare where each document part begins (chapter breaks) and which page layout to use for each document part. We're using the term "document part" to mean each major section, such as a title, Table of Contents, chapter, glossary, or index. Flare uses the term "chapter" generically to refer to these document parts.

In this task, you'll link the applicable page layout to the first topic in each chapter. When you build your output, Flare uses that layout for the remaining topics until it encounters another chapter break.

In addition, if you have TOC entries for topics within a chapter, you need to link only the first TOC entry that uses the page layout you are assigning to that chapter.

Let's look at the TOC outline you created in Task 2.

Notice that you *don't* need to link the topics called "Overview" and "Starting your application" to page layouts because they will use the page layout called "Chapter Pg Layout," which is linked to the Chapter 1 topic. Also notice that you *do* need to link the first topic in Chapter 2 to "Chapter Pg Layout," but you don't need to link its second topic, "Adding accounts."

Okay, let's see how to set chapter breaks and link to page layouts.

1. In the Project Organizer, expand the **TOCs** folder and double-click **Outline for PDF output (Master)**.

2. In the TOC Editor, select **Title**, then **Run Properties Dialog for this item** ▣ on the top toolbar. The Properties dialog opens.

3. Select the **Printed Output** tab.

This section applies to master pages only. You don't need it if you're using page layouts.

4. In the Chapter Break section, check **Start a new chapter document** to create the chapter break. You must check this box in order to assign a page layout to this TOC entry.

5. In the Configure chapter using this Page Layout section, select **Title Pg Layout**.

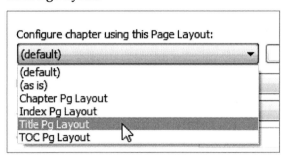

6. From the Page Type list, select **First**. (This is the page type we want Flare to use for the first page of the Title "chapter.")

7. Leave Auto-end on 'left' page set to **Enabled**.

8. In the Page Number section, select **Reset to** and verify that the number is **1**. Then select **roman (i, ii, iii)** from the Format list.

9. Click **OK**.

10. You do the rest, using the following chart for help.

For TOC entry ...	Assign page layout ...	Select page type ...	Set the page numbers to ...
Contents	TOC Pg Layout	Right	Continue from previous
Chapter 1	Chapter Pg Layout	Right	Reset to 1 Format: Decimal (1, 2, 3)
Chapter 2	Chapter Pg Layout	Right	Continue from previous
Index	Index Pg Layout	Right	Continue from previous

Notice that you're using "Right" for the page type. That's because you want each chapter to start on an odd page. By selecting "Right," you're telling Flare to use the Right page type for the first page of each chapter.

11. Click **Save All** 🗐 to save your work.

12. Close the TOC.

TASK 8: SET UP THE PRINT TARGET

Now you'll tell Flare what you want to build—your print output. This is done by setting up the print target. You're almost there!

1. In the Project Organizer, expand **Targets** and double-click **MyPDF (Primary)**. The MyPDF target opens in the Target Editor.

2. Click the **Basic** tab (if not already visible).

3. When you created your project, you should have selected PDF as the output type. If you didn't, select **PDF** as the Output Type now.

4. In the Master TOC field, select **Outline for PDF output**. (That's your topic outline.)

    For this tutorial, no other options need to be set.

5. Click **Save All** to save your work.

6. Click **x** on the MyPDF tab to close the Target Editor.

    Because you saved the target settings, you can build your output at any time, even immediately. Let's try that now.

TASK 9: BUILD THE PRINT OUTPUT

Building the print output is the easiest part of this process. Although it's the last task before distributing your output, you'll likely build your output many times before you're done setting up layouts and developing your project's content.

> ***Tip*** — Build your output as you set up your page layouts, so you can see the results and make sure that you're getting what you want.

1. In the Project Organizer, under Targets, right-click **MyPDF (Primary)** and select **Build 'MyPDF'** from the menu.

A Build Progress window opens as Flare builds the output for the target you selected. If your project is large, this might take several seconds.

2. Click **Yes** to view the output when prompted. Your default PDF viewer opens and displays the output you built.

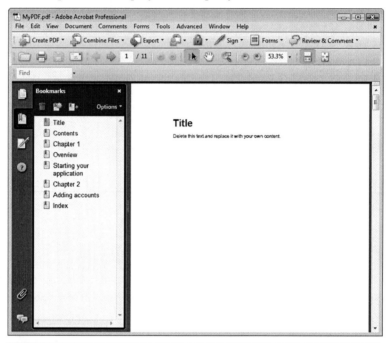

> **Note** — If you look at the Contents and Index pages in the PDF file, you'll notice a thin black line above the Table of Contents and index entries. This tutorial uses styles from Flare's "Styles.css" stylesheet. In the Styles stylesheet, the styles for proxies (used in the index and Table of Contents) are set up to have a one-pixel black line at the beginning of the proxy content. If you want to change this, see "Editing styles" in the Flare Help system.

Congratulations! You've survived the construction of a more complex output document!

When you're ready to distribute your PDF file, you'll find it in a folder under your project's Output folder. The file is in a folder named for the target you built (**MyPDF** in this tutorial).

To view and distribute other types of print output, see "Types of print output" on page 180.

LEARN MORE

This section contains more information about the features you used in the tutorial part of this chapter. Refer to it as needed.

THE INDEX PROXY DIALOG

When you create a topic for an index (Task 1: Create placeholder topics on page 193), if you insert an index proxy, the Index Proxy dialog opens. This section describes more about the options on this dialog.

> **Note** — With Flare Version 4.2, you don't need to insert an index proxy if you select the **TopicForIndex** template when you create the topic.

Figure 5A-6: Index Proxy dialog

Table 5A-3:
Options on
the Index
Proxy
dialog

In this field ...	Do the following ...
Generate Headings	Accept the default, which includes headings (such as A, B, C) for index entries, or select **No** if you don't want index headings.
Column Count	Accept the default, which is two columns, or select the number of columns you want your index to have.
Header Height (*Applies to FrameMaker only*)	Accept the default ("not set"), or type the amount of space you want between the index header and the index entries.
Stylesheet class for proxy element	Leave this field blank to use the default style for your index.
	Note — You will not see any classes listed here unless you already created stylesheet classes (an advanced feature not covered in this book). If you need to create styles for your print indexes, search the Flare Help system for "classes" and look for a topic called "Creating New Style Classes."

PAGE LAYOUTS

In Flare, a **page layout** is a file you create to specify the layout for the pages in a part of your document. You'll create one layout for each unique combination of these page characteristics, including:

- Page orientation
- Page size
- Page number format
- Whether to include a header on the first page
- Header contents and placement
- Footer contents and placement

For many writers, this means creating one layout for each of the following document parts:

- Title page

- Table of contents

- Chapter (one page layout for each *different* chapter format)

- Glossary

- Index

> ***Important***— Prior to Flare Version 4.0, master pages were used to define the format for print output. With Version 4.0, MadCap added page layouts, which provide greater functionality and flexibility in defining the layout of pages. You now have two choices for defining page layouts. MadCap recommends using page layouts for print output and master pages to add headers and footers to topics in online output.

Page layout templates

To simplify print output, Flare includes templates for standard page layouts. You'll create a page layout by using one of these templates as a starting point. (These are not the same as *topic* templates, which you use when creating a new topic.)

Flare provides the following page-layout templates.

Table 5A-4: Flare page-layout templates

Page-layout template	Use this template for ...
ChapterA4	Page sizes that conform to the A4 international standard, which is 21 x 29.7 cm (8.27 x 11.69 in.).
ChapterLegal	Legal documents (page size is 8.5 x 14 in.).
ChapterLetter	Letter-size documents (page size is 8.5 x 11 in.). Frames in this layout are not anchored.
ChapterResizable	Letter-size documents (page size is 8.5 x 11 in.) that use frames. Frames are anchored.*
Default	The body of a document or simple letter-size documents that need a header, body, and footer. Margins are set to one inch all around.

Page-layout template	Use this template for ...
FrontMatterResizable	Front matter pages, such as Tables of Contents (page size is 8.5 x 11 in.). Frames are anchored.*
GlossaryResizable	Glossaries (page size is 8.5 x 11 in.). Frames are anchored.*
IndexResizable	Indexes (page size is 8.5 x 11 in.). This option includes the variables "Heading.FirstIndexTerm" and "Heading.LastIndexTerm" in the header. These variables are available only for PDF, XPS, and XHTML output. Frames are anchored.*
NormalResizable	The body of a document or simple letter-size documents that need a header, body, and footer. This option is identical to the "default" layout except that frames are anchored.* Margins are set to one inch all around.

Table 5A-4:
(Cont.)

* Anchored frames maintain their distance from the edge of the page if you change the page size of the layout.

Page types

For each page layout, you can define six different types of pages (First, Right, Left, Title, Normal, and Empty). The page buttons on the right represent each page type contained in a page layout.

Figure 5A-7:
*Page layout
showing
frames and
page types*

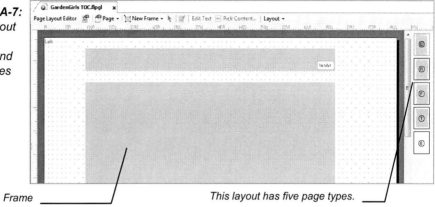

Frame _____   *This layout has five page types.* _____

Page buttons

Clicking a page button opens that page in the Page Layout Editor.

Table 5A-5:
*Page
Layout
Editor Page
buttons*

This button ...	Opens ...
(L)	The Left page type.
(R)	The Right page type.
(F)	The First page type.
(T)	The Title page type.
(N)	The Normal page type.
(E)	The Empty page type.

Page frames

Each page type contains **frames** that act as placeholders for content. Page layouts can contain these types of frames:

- Header

- Footer

- Body

- Decoration (not supported by Word or FrameMaker)

- Image

Frames also indicate where the content should be placed on the printed page. To arrange content, you can insert, move, and resize frames. You can also set up a frame's characteristics. For example, a frame can have one or more columns, a background color, and borders.

There is much more you can do with frames in Flare. We're just scratching the surface to get you started.

> ***Note*** — As of the writing of this book, there are still some issues with print output headers, empty page padding, and page number formats. It's likely that those issues will be resolved with a future release of Flare. However, if you produce Word or FrameMaker output, you can easily fix these things with those applications after building your output.

Editing frames

You can edit the contents of all frames except body frames. You edit frames in the Frame Contents window, which has some of the same features as the XML Editor.

Body frames

You cannot change the content of body frames. When you build your output, Flare automatically places your topic content into the body frames.

However, you can insert more body frames on a page to control the flow of content and how it is formatted.

Arrows indicate the direction in which the
text flows from one body frame to another.

Figure 5A-8:
Multiple
body
frames on
a page

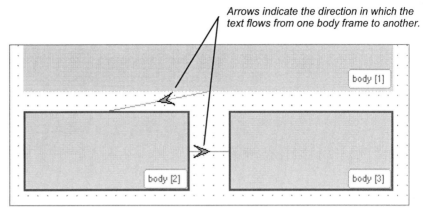

Header and footer frames

You set up header and footer frames with the content you want. To get content into headers and footers:

- Type text into them

- Insert snippets

- Insert variables (such as page numbers or heading text from topics)

THE PROPERTIES DIALOG

This section provides more detail about the Printed Output tab of the Properties dialog that you use to link TOC entries to page layouts. You'll use this dialog only when creating more complex documents such as documents that contain front and back matter. See "Task 7: Link page layouts to topics in the TOC" on page 213.

This dialog can be confusing if you don't understand the fields it contains.

To open the Properties dialog:

Do one of the following:

- Right-click the TOC item whose properties you want to view and select **Properties** from the menu.

- Select the TOC item whose properties you want to view and click **Run Properties Dialog for this item** .

The Printed Output tab of the Properties dialog has two sections— each used with a different and mutually exclusive Flare feature:

- **Section Break** (top section) is used with master pages.

- **Chapter Break** (bottom section) is used with page layouts.

The page layout feature was introduced with Version 4.0 of Flare. Because page layouts provide more options and greater flexibility for creating print output than master pages, MadCap recommends that you use page layouts for creating print output if you have Version 4.0 or later.

This section is for Flare users who used **master pages** to create print output with older versions of Flare.

Figure 5A-9:
Properties dialog, Printed Output tab

This section is for Flare users who use **page layouts** to create print output (Flare Version 4.0 and later).

> **Note** — For Word documents, when you check **Start a new chapter document** in the above dialog, Flare inserts a section break before the chapter whose properties you are setting up. The section break is Odd or Even depending on if you selected Right or Left respectively for the Page Type on this dialog.

WHY PRIMARY TARGETS MATTER

Your project can have many targets, but one target is always designated as "primary." "Primary target" is Flare's way of singling out one target. Why is this important?

When you're viewing topics in the XML Editor window in *print layout mode*, Flare uses the primary target's settings to determine what you see. For example, if the primary target uses a page layout, you'll see that layout's headers and footers in the XML Editor. For more information about viewing topics in print layout mode, see "Task 7: Viewing layout modes" on page 84.

For convenience, Flare provides toolbar buttons to open, build, view, or publish the primary target. You may find these buttons easier to use if you work more with one target than others.

> **Note** — To change which target is primary, right-click the target in the Project Organizer and select **Make Primary** from the menu.

WHAT'S NEXT?

At this point, you could continue adding content to your project. Since setup is done, you can also re-build the document at any time. Just remember:

- **If you add topics to your project**, you must add linked TOC entries for those topics.

- **If any of those topics will begin a new chapter**, you must designate them as chapter breaks in the TOC and link them to page layouts (see Task 7 starting on page 213).

You've now gone through an entire project cycle, from creating the project to building output! If you keep working with Flare and try other, more advanced features, it won't be long before you're a bona fide Propeller Head or even a Propellus Maximus (these are titles granted to frequent posters on the Flare user forum).

In addition:

- If you want to develop online output, take a look at Step 5B: Create Online Output.

- If you want to explore other features of Flare, check out the appendixes.

Step 5B:
Create
Online Output

STEP 5: Create Output
5A: Print Output
5B: Online Output

STEP 4:
Create
Nav Aids

STEP 3:
Develop
Content

STEP 2:
Learn the
XML Editor

STEP 1:
Get Started

In this chapter ...

➤ Learn about types of online output
➤ Add breadcrumbs
➤ Add a master page
➤ Set up a target
➤ Build online output
➤ Test and troubleshoot
➤ Distribute online output

OVERVIEW

This step explains how to create and distribute online output, such as Help systems and knowledge bases.

Before you begin using the procedures in this chapter, make sure you have done the following:

- **Create your project**. Any Flare project can be created as online output. To create the project, see "Creating a Flare project" on page 39.

- **Create and format your content**. You create content and format for online output as you would for any other output as described in Step 2: Learn the XML Editor, and Step 3: Develop Content.

- **Add navigation aids**. Use Step 4: Create Navigation Aids, to add links and create index entries for navigation.

> ***Note*** — If you're unfamiliar with terms and concepts such as *output, build, distribute* and *target,* refer to the Document Basics chapter.

KEEPING TRACK OF ONLINE OUTPUT

To make it easier to track various targets and types of output, we've created a Target Settings form (see Appendix A). As you learn to create more targets for your output, you'll find it very helpful to record the names of various Flare project files.

We suggest that you keep a copy of this form handy as you proceed through this chapter and begin making it a habit to fill it out.

TYPES OF ONLINE OUTPUT

With Flare, you can create the following types of online output.

Table 5B-1:
Types of online output

Output Type	Description
DotNet Help	A Help format created by MadCap Software (Figure 5B-1).
	For more information, see "About DotNet Help Output" in Flare's Help system.
HTML Help	An HTML-based Help format created by Microsoft that is used to develop Help systems for Windows desktop applications (Figure 5B-2).
	For more information, see "About HTML Help Output" in Flare's Help system.
WebHelp	A web-based Help format that can be run on any Internet browser or platform (Figure 5B-3).
	For more information, see "About WebHelp Output" in Flare's Help system.
WebHelp AIR	A web-based Help format created by Adobe that can be run via a single file from a desktop rather than a server (Figure 5B-4 and Figure 5B-5).
	To create online documents in WebHelp AIR:
	▪ You and users must install Abobe AIR (go to http://get.adobe.com/air/ for a free download).
	▪ You must install Java Runtime Environment (go to http://java.sun.com/javase/downloads/index.jsp for a free download).
	For more information, see "About WebHelp AIR Output" in Flare's Help system.
WebHelp Plus	A web-based Help format that provides enhanced functionality (Figure 5B-6).
	For more information, see "About WebHelp Plus Output" in Flare's Help system.

Figure 5B-1:
DotNet
Help
sample

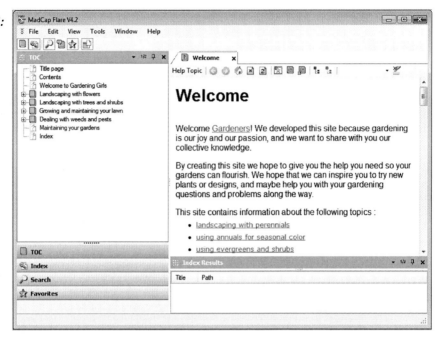

Figure 5B-2:
HTML
Help
sample

Figure 5B-3:
WebHelp
sample

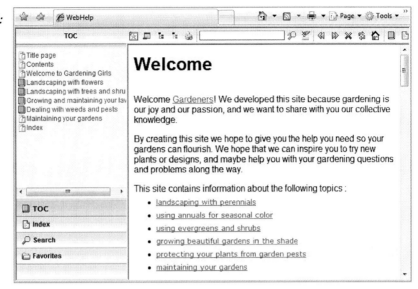

Figure 5B-4:
WebHelp
AIR sample

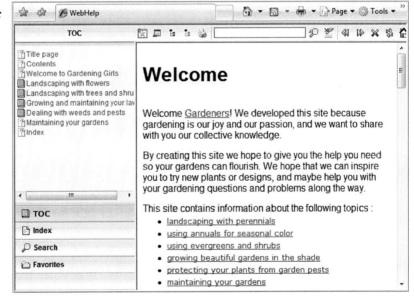

WebHelp AIR output is in one file

Figure 5B-5:
WebHelp
AIR output
in Windows
Explorer

Figure 5B-6:
WebHelp
Plus sample

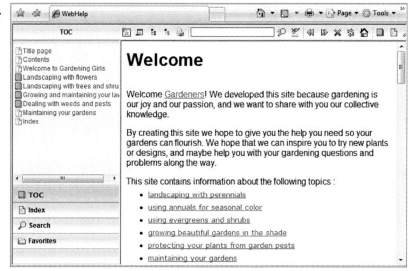

THE BASIC STEPS

Here's a list of the steps you'll take to create online output:

- Create a TOC. See "Creating a Table of Contents" on page 144.

- Add index keywords in topics. See "Creating index entries" on page 171.

- (*Optional*) Add a master page to include a header, footer, and breadcrumbs in your online output.

- Set up your target.

- Build your online output.

- Test and troubleshoot.

- Distribute online output.

> ***Note*** — When creating online output, you may want to create browse sequences, which are a type of navigation aid. To learn about them, search the Flare Help system for "browse sequences."

ABOUT BREADCRUMBS

Breadcrumbs are an optional navigation aid. The Breadcrumbs show the path through the TOC to the topic currently open in a Help system session. The breadcrumb trail appears just above the open topic in the output as shown in the following screen.

Figure 5B-7:
Breadcrumb
trail

breadcrumbs

To show breadcrumbs, you must use a breadcrumbs proxy in a master page and select that master page when you set up your target. If you add a master page to your project (described next) by selecting the MasterPage Factory Template, you automatically get a breadcrumbs proxy.

> ***Note*** — If you don't want the breadcrumb trail, simply delete it from the master page. From the Content Explorer's Resources\MasterPages folder, open the master page, right-click the proxy, and select **Edit** → **Delete**.

ADDING A MASTER PAGE

Master pages let you add headers, footers, and breadcrumbs to
multiple topics in online output.

To add a master page:

1. Select **Project → Add Master Page**. The Add New Master Page
    dialog opens.

2. In the Templates section, select **MasterPage.flmsp** to create a
    master page. (The breadcrumbs proxy is automatically used with
    this template.)

3. In the File name field, type a name for the master page.

> **Best Practice** — Record the name of the Master Page on the Target
> Settings form provided in Appendix A.

4. Click **Add**, then **OK** to copy the master page.

The master page file (.flmsp) is added to the
Resources\MasterPages folder in the Content Explorer and the
XML Editor opens with the new master page shown.

5. (*Optional*) To include a header in your topics, place your cursor
    before the topic body proxy and type text or include content.
    (You can place it either before or after the breadcrumbs proxy.)

> **Note** — You can insert any type of content in headers and footers,
> including images, snippets, variables, and even text hyperlinks.

6. (*Optional*) To include a footer in your topics, place your cursor
    after the **mini-toc proxy** and type text or include content.

7. (*Optional*) To remove a proxy from the master page, right-click it,
    then select **Edit → Delete**.

8. Click **Save All** to save your work.

    After you create a master page, you must select it when you set
    up your target, (next page).

> **Note** — You can add multiple master pages to your project, but you can
> associate only one master page with each target in your project.

EDITING A SKIN

A skin defines the appearance of online output—its interface. A skin
file stores the interface settings, such as the buttons that will appear,
colors, and accordion bars (or tabs if HTML Help).

Creating a skin is an advanced feature not covered in this book, but we can tell you how to edit a skin.

 To edit a skin:

1. Open the Project Organizer.

2. Expand the Skins folder.

3. Double-click the skin you want to edit. The Skin Editor opens.

4. Select the interface features you want (such as Table of Contents, Index, Search, and Favorites) and the buttons you want (such as Back, Forward, Home).

5. On the Styles tab, change styles as desired (colors, fonts, etc.) for the parts of the interface (accordions, buttons, text, background colors, etc.).

   Here's an example of HTML Help.

With the Skin Editor, you can choose which buttons you want to appear here.

Figure 5B-8:
Example of an HTML Help skin

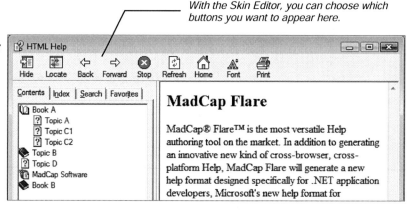

For more information about using skins, search for "skins" in the Flare Help system.

SETTING UP AN ONLINE TARGET

Now that you've finished creating the online content, TOC, and index keywords, you'll tell Flare what you want to build—the output. You do this by setting up an online target.

PRIMARY TARGETS

Your project can have many targets, but one target is always designated as "primary." "Primary target" is Flare's way of singling out one target so you can use toolbar buttons to open, build, view, or publish that target. You may find this easier if you work more with one target than others.

> **Note** — Primary targets matter when viewing topics in print layout mode. For more information, see "Why primary targets matter" on page 227.

Use the following procedure to set up a target.

 To set up a target:

1. In the Project Organizer, expand the **Targets** folder and double-click the target you want to set up.

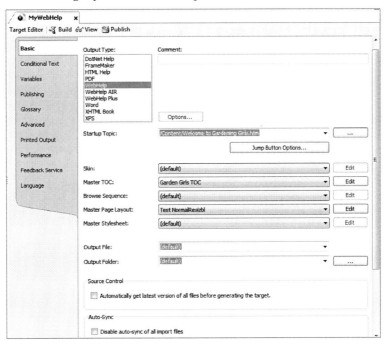

2. Click the **Basic** tab to open it (if necessary).

3. When you created your project, you should have selected the desired online output type. If you didn't, select the Output Type

now. (See "Types of online output" on page 231 for online
output types.)

> **Best Practice** — Record the target name on the Target Settings form in
> Appendix A.

4. In the Startup Topic field, select the topic you want opened
    when a user opens the online output.

5. In the Master TOC field, select the desired TOC for this target.

> **Best Practice** — Record the TOC for this target on the Target Settings
> form in Appendix A.

6. In the Master Stylesheet field, select the stylesheet used to apply
    styles to this target. If you select **default**, the Styles stylesheet
    will be used with this target.

7. In the Output File field, type a name for the file that will launch
    the online output (Help system or knowledge base).

> **Best Practice** — Check with the software developer to see if there are
> any requirements for the Output File name. If not, an easy way to keep
> track of your projects is to enter your project name and the target type (plus
> the appropriate file extension) as your Output File name.
> Example: "YourProjectWebHelp.htm"
>
> Don't forget to record the name of the Output File on the Target Settings
> form in Appendix A. You'll need to remember its name when you distribute
> your output.

In Flare, the Output File is also called the Main Entry file. For
RoboHelp™ users, this is the start page.

8. (*Optional*) If you are creating a target for online output that
    contains conditional text, click the **Conditional Text** tab.

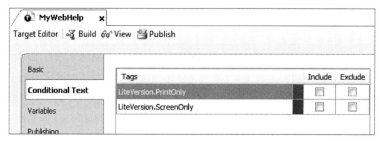

On this tab, check the condition tags you want to include and exclude in your target.

> **Important** — Unless excluded, all content tagged with a condition tag *is automatically included* in output.
>
> **Best Practice** — Make explicit choices on this tab. Check what you want to include *and* check what you want to exclude.

9. (*Optional*) If you are using variables in your topics, click the **Variables** tab to change the value of variables for this target only.

10. (*Optional*) If you are creating a target for context-sensitive help, click the **Advanced** tab and select an Alias File. See "Adding an alias file" on page 310.

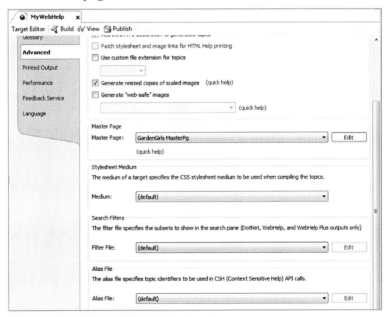

11. (*Optional*) If you are using a master page, click the **Advanced** tab and select the Master Page you want to use to build this target.

12. Click **Save All** 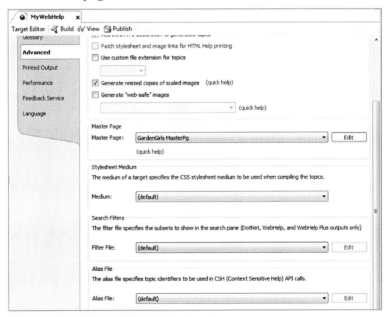 to save your work.

Because you saved the target settings, you can build the online output at any time, even immediately. Let's try that now.

BUILDING ONLINE OUTPUT

Building online output is a snap. However, you'll probably build
often as you develop content to see how it will look.

> **Best Practice** — Build frequently, especially when you're using condition
> tags. Doing so will help you verify that the TOC structure is working—plus you
> can correct any broken links as you develop content.

To build online output:

1. In the Project Organizer, under Targets, right-click the desired
   target and select **Build 'target name'** from the menu.

   A Build Progress window opens as Flare builds the output
   according to the selections you made. If your project is large, this
   might take several seconds.

2. Click **Yes** to view the output when prompted. Your online
   output is displayed. Here's a sample of WebHelp output on a
   computer running Windows Vista.

Nice work!

For samples of how your online output will look, see "Types of online output" on page 231.

TESTING AND TROUBLESHOOTING

When you built your output, Flare checked it for errors. During a build, errors will be listed in the Build Progress window.

One of the most common types of errors is broken links. This and other problems are described in Appendix E: Troubleshoot, which starts on page 317, along with information about using the internal analyzer that comes with Flare.

When you make any changes to your content, remember to re-build your output.

> *Best Practice* — Always test your links after building online output to verify that they connect to the correct content.

WHAT IS PUBLISHING?

Publishing is *optional*. It is simply is a way of distributing online output—typically WebHelp—after it is built. When you publish, you define a destination where Flare should place the output. The destination can be a website, Intranet location, FTP server, or local hard drive folder. You define that destination from the Publishing tab of the Target Editor.

We discourage the use of publishing for beginners unless you are publishing to your local hard drive! It is much safer to distribute online files manually as we describe than to place them directly on the Web. Besides, software developers and webmasters might prefer that you *not* copy files directly to the web server. Read on to learn about alternatives to publishing.

DISTRIBUTING ONLINE OUTPUT

Distributing your output simply means sending your project to others after it is built. However, *how* you distribute and *what* you distribute differs depending on the type of output you have created and your preferences.

HOW TO DISTRIBUTE

In most cases, you will provide the software developer with the output files so they can be linked to an application. When using the application, users will access your output via the Help menu or context-sensitive help buttons.

With Flare, you can distribute online output in these ways:

- By using an FTP application to upload output files to an FTP site.

- By using Windows Explorer to copy output to another location, such as a folder on a network. This method is quick and easy!

- By burning your output files to a CD.

- By publishing your output to a website or Intranet location (not recommended for beginners) or to a hard drive. See "What is publishing?" previously for details.

WHAT TO DISTRIBUTE

To distribute your output, you must supply:

- The name of the Output File (the file that launches the online output—defined when you created the target). See "Setting up an online target" on page 238 for details.

- Specific files and folders as defined in Table 5B-2.

> **Note** — You distribute only *output* files; you don't distribute your project's source files (the files contained in the Content folder under your project name).

Use Table 5B-2 as a guide to when you're ready to distribute your output.

Table 5B-2:	To distribute ...	Include ...
What to distribute	DotNet Help	All *output* files and folders under Ouput\<your user name>, starting with the folder named for the target, plus the MadCap Help Viewer (a free download from MadCap Software).
	HTML Help	The CHM file (such as YourProject.chm).
	WebHelp	All *output* files and folders under Ouput\<your user name>, starting with the folder named for the target.
	WebHelp Plus	All *output* files and folders under Ouput\<your user name>, starting with the folder named for the target.
	WebHelp AIR	The AIR file (such as YourProject.air). Users must also install Adobe AIR™ (a free download at http://get.adobe.com/air/).

Where are the project's output files?

Here is where you can find your project's output files if you use the default locations for storing your project files.

- **For Vista** — In Windows Explorer, open the **My Projects** folder in the **Documents** folder. The output files for each target are located in the Output folder under your project name.

  Example:
  Documents\My Projects\Gardening Girls\Output\<user name>\<target name>

- **For XP** — In Windows Explorer, open the **My Projects** folder in the **My Documents** folder. The output files for each target are located in the Output folder under your project name.

Figure 5B-9:
Default
location of
project
output as
seen in
Windows
Explorer

About the Output File

The Output File was created when you defined the target. This is the file that launches your online output. The Output File uses the following file extensions:

Table 5B-3:
Output
File
extensions

Extension	Type of output
.mchelp	DotNet Help
.chm	HTML Help
.htm	WebHelp and WebHelp Plus
.air	WebHelp AIR

You'll need to give the software developer the name of the Output File and its location. The application needs to run this file.

For each type of online output listed above, you can find the Output File in the following folder (if you accepted the default project location when you created your project):

My Projects\<project name>\Output\<user name\<target name>

WHAT'S NEXT?

At this point, you could continue adding content to your project. Since setup is done, you can also re-build the document at any time. Just remember that **if you add topics to your project, you must add linked TOC entries for those topics**.

You've now gone through an entire project cycle, from creating the project to building output! If you keep working with Flare and try other, more advanced features, it won't be long before you're a bona fide Propeller Head or even a Propellus Maximus (these are titles granted to frequent posters on the Flare user forum).

In addition:

- If you want to develop print output, take a look at Step 5A: Create Print Output.

- If you want to explore other features of Flare, check out the appendixes.

Appendix A: Planning Worksheets

In this chapter …

PART 1: SOURCE OF CONTENT

Use this worksheet to define where your content will come from. Copy this worksheet as needed.

If your content is …	Decide …
Not in electronic form	• Which topics will you create? _____ _____ _____ _____ • Which images will you create? _____ _____ _____
Word or FrameMaker documents	How will you maintain the content? ☐ By using Flare ☐ By using your source application If maintaining with source application, do you want Flare to *automatically* re-import? (The alternative is that *you initiate* the re-importing.) ☐ Yes ☐ No
HTML files	Do you want to keep the style of your source content or use a Flare stylesheet? ☐ Keep style of source content ☐ Use a Flare stylesheet Name of Flare stylesheet: _____

PART 2: TYPE OF OUTPUT

Use this worksheet to define the output to be built by Flare. Copy this worksheet as needed.

To create …	Decide …
Online output	● Type of output: (*Check all that apply. Indicate if you want to create multiple outputs of one type—for different versions, etc.*) ☐ WebHelp ☐ HTML Help ☐ WebHelp Plus ☐ DotNet Help ☐ WebHelp AIR ● How will you structure the Help TOC (books, sub-books, with topics in each)? We recommend that you write this structure on a separate sheet and list the topics in each. ● Which images will you include? (*Use a separate page as needed.*) _____ _____ _____ ● How do you want your final output to look? Body text font: _____ Size: _____ Color: _____ Heading 1 font: _____ Size: _____ Color: _____ Heading 2 font: _____ Size: _____ Color: _____ ● Which interface (skin) will you use? ☐ Default Help interface ☐ Custom interface (not covered in this book) Name: _____ Location: _____ ● (WebHelp only) Which buttons do you want on the toolbar? _____ ● (HTML Help only) Which Help buttons do you want? _____ ● Which features do you want? (TOC, Index, Search, etc.) _____ (Features appear as tabs in HTML Help and as accordion bars in other types of Help.)

To create …	Decide …
Print output	■ Type of output: ☐ Word document ☐ FrameMaker document ☐ PDF file ☐ XPS file* (requires either Vista, Microsoft .NET Framework 3.0, or Word 2007 with the Office 2007 "Save as XPS" add-in) ☐ XHTML file* ■ For the output selected above, choose which of the following will be included: ☐ TOC ☐ Mini-TOC ☐ Glossary ☐ Endnotes ☐ List of concepts ☐ List of elements (table of figures or images) ☐ First page header: _____ ☐ Right page header: _____ ☐ Left page header: _____ ☐ First page footer: _____ ☐ Right page footer: _____ ☐ Left page footer: _____ *(If you checked multiple front and back matter parts, you might need a separate page to document the headers and footers for each part.)* Start each document part on the right (odd) side? ☐ Yes _____ ☐ No End each document part on a left page that is empty if necessary? ☐ Yes _____ ☐ No ■ For the output selected above, identify: Page size: _____ Page orientation: ☐ Portrait ☐ Landscape Page margins: Left: _____ Right : _____ Top: _____ Bottom: _____ Unit of measure (inches, pixels, points, etc.): _____

* Flare version 4.0 and later.

PART 3: CONTENT REVIEWS

Use this worksheet to determine how content will be reviewed. Copy this worksheet as needed.

Select one	If reviewers use ...	Reviews will proceed like this ...
☐	Flare or X-Edit (Full, Contribute or Review)*	▪ You send reviewers Flare topics. ▪ Reviewers view topics with Flare or X-Edit and annotate them. ▪ You view comments in Flare and accept or dismiss them in your Flare topics.
☐	Word or FrameMaker	▪ You give reviewers Word or FrameMaker documents in electronic or print forms that contain the topics to be reviewed. ▪ You type changes directly into your Flare topics.
☐	Printed documents	▪ You print topics from Flare or give reviewers a PDF that contains the topics to be reviewed. ▪ You type changes directly into your Flare topics.

* Recommended.

PART 4: START NEW PROJECT

Use this worksheet before you begin using the Start New Project Wizard. Copy this worksheet as needed.

Note — If you choose to create the project and import the content simultaneously, you do not need to use the Start New Project Wizard. For simplicity, we don't cover that feature in this guide. However, the Flare Help system does an excellent job describing how to use it. Just search for "Creating a project by importing."

If you want to …	Decide …
Store your project in a location other than the default folder *Note* — The Windows XP default is My Documents\My Projects. The Windows Vista default is <user name>\Documents\My Projects.	Where your project will be stored: _____ _____
Use your project with a source control application	Identify the type of source control application: ☐ Visual Source Safe Location of INI file: _____ Folder used to store Flare project: _____ ☐ Team Foundation Server Location: _____ ☐ Other: _____ Location: _____

PART 5: TARGET SETTINGS

Use this form to record the settings for the target to be built by Flare. Copy this form as needed.

Product Names/Acronyms:

Target	Master TOC	"Master" Page Layout	Master Page (Advanced tab)	Medium	Condition Tags	Output File (Main Entry File)
					Incl: Excl:	
					Incl: Excl:	
					Incl: Excl:	
					Incl: Excl:	
					Incl: Excl:	
					Incl: Excl:	

Sample Target Settings Form (Two Products)

Product Names/Acronyms: Widget Professional (WPRO) Widget Home (WHME)   Both products (WIDG)

Target	Master TOC	"Master" Page Layout	Master Page (Advanced tab)	Medium	Conditionals	Output File (Main Entry File)
WPRO PDF	WPRO Print TOC	WIDG Pg Layout	—	WIDG PrintMed	**Excl:** Comments, WHome, Online	WPRO help topics.pdf
WPRO WebHelp	WPRO Online TOC	—	WIDG Master Page	—	**Excl:** Comments, Print WHome.	WPRO Ver2-1 Help.htm
WPRO Word	WPRO Print TOC	WIDG Pg Layout	—	WIDG PrintMed	**Excl:** Comments, Online WHome.	WPRO help topics.doc
WHME PDF	WHME Print TOC	WIDG Pg Layout	—	WIDG PrintMed	**Excl:** Comments, WPro, Online	WHME help topics.pdf
WHME WebHelp	WHME Online TOC	—	WIDG Master Page	—	**Excl:** Comments & WPro, Print	WHME Ver2-1 Help.htm
WHME Word	WHME Print TOC	WIDG Pg Layout	—	WIDG PrintMed	**Excl:** Comments, WPro, Online	WHME help topics.doc

Stylesheet for all: WIDG Help Styles

Startup topic for WPRO and WHME WebHelp: Welcome

Skin for WPRO and WHME WebHelp: WIDG Skin

Appendix B:
Import
Content

In this chapter ...
> What you can import
> Import Word and Frame files
> Import HTML files

OVERVIEW

In Step1: Get Started, you learned how to create content (topics) from scratch. Now you'll learn how to import content into a Flare project. Not only is importing a fast way to add content, but it also makes the most sense if content already exists. Why re-create content if you don't have to?

You can import content into Flare:

- By creating a Flare project to hold the content and then importing the content, or

- By creating a Flare project and importing the content at the same time.

Since you've already learned how to create a Flare project, we'll discuss only the first scenario. Let's start by looking at what you can import into Flare.

WHAT YOU CAN IMPORT

You can import these documents into Flare:

- Microsoft Word documents, 2003 and newer (DOC, DOCX, and RTF files)

- Adobe FrameMaker documents (BOOK, FM, and MIF files)

- HTML files

- RoboHelp projects (MPG and XPJ files)

- XHTML files (from other Flare projects)

- Microsoft HTML Help projects (HHP files)

When Flare imports content, it converts it to XHTML format.

> **Note** — You can also import an existing Flare project from a source control application.

WHAT THIS APPENDIX INCLUDES

In this appendix, we'll cover three import options:

- Importing Word files

- Importing FrameMaker files

- Importing HTML files

You may also find it handy to copy and paste small pieces of text into your topics, which is done without importing. See "Copying and pasting text into a topic" on page 98 for details.

WHAT YOU WON'T FIND IN THIS APPENDIX

As we said earlier, this book addresses the needs of new Flare users who have little experience with document authoring tools.

Consequently, we don't discuss how to do these tasks:

- **Import a RoboHelp project**. RoboHelp users transitioning to Flare can find instructions by searching for "robohelp project" in the Flare Help system.

- **Import XHTML files from another Flare project**. For information, search for "importing xhtml" in the Flare Help system.

- **Link project files from other Flare projects** (an exciting feature called "global project linking" introduced in Version 4.0). To learn about this feature, search for "global project linking" in the Flare Help system.

GETTING STARTED

It's likely that you have Word, FrameMaker, or HTML files, but not all three to import. So there's no need to read this entire appendix.

Use this chart to help you decide which sections to read.

Table B-1: *What sections to read*

If you have ...	Do this ...	See these sections ...
Content in Word files	Import the Word files Use heading styles to break the content into topics	Importing from Word and FrameMaker files, next A bird's-eye view of the import process (page 261) Dividing one document into many topics (page 263) Choices for importing styles (page 264) Choices for maintaining content (page 265) Importing a Word document (page 267)
Content in FrameMaker files	Import the FrameMaker files Use heading styles to break the content into topics	Importing from Word and FrameMaker files (page 260) A bird's-eye view of the import process (page 261) Dividing one document into many topics (page 263) Choices for importing styles (page 264) Choices for maintaining content (page 265) Importing a FrameMaker document (page 275)
Content in HTM or HTML files (such as website content)	Copy and paste the files into your project	Importing HTML files (page 286)

IMPORTING FROM WORD AND FRAMEMAKER FILES

With some import programs, you simply transfer text and start maintaining it in its new form. You can do this with Flare, but we suggest you consider using one of Flare's most powerful features: linking Flare topics to the program (source) that created them.

What does this mean? It means you can **import content from Word or FrameMaker and then update it in Word or FrameMaker.** That's it!

When source and destination files are linked, you can re-import the content at any time or choose to have Flare automatically check for updates to the source. The bottom line is that you don't have to use Flare's XML Editor to make updates if you prefer doing so in Word or FrameMaker.

A BIRD'S-EYE VIEW OF THE IMPORT PROCESS

Now that you know what's possible, let's take a high-level look at the entire process, starting with what to do before you import the content.

Before importing

DECISION TIME!

Before you import a document, decide:

✓ Which documents will you import?

✓ Where do you want to divide the content into topics?

✓ How do you want Flare to handle styles when it converts your Word or FrameMaker documents?

✓ Will you maintain the content with Flare or with your original source program (Word or FrameMaker)?

After you've made these decisions, **prepare your content for importing.** The cleaner your source files are, the smoother the import will be. We suggest that you take these steps:

- **Use styles to control formatting** rather than local formatting. Don't use toolbar buttons and shortcut keys to apply formatting such as bold and italics.

- **Clean up the styles in your Word or FrameMaker document** (if necessary). It's easy to have a proliferation of style variations.

See "Choices for importing styles" on page 264 for more information about why this is important.

- **Make sure that the text of each topic is contiguous**. Choose a paragraph style (typically a heading style) that will be used to divide topics in Flare. Then edit your document to make sure that *the content of each topic* is preceded by that heading style. See "Dividing one document into many topics" to learn more.

> ***Important*** — The time you invest in cleaning up your content upfront is worth it! It will mean fewer surprises when you import it.

Flare import tasks

Importing content from Word or FrameMaker into Flare is a two-part process:

- First, you'll **set up the rules** for importing the content. This involves telling Flare the decisions you made about importing, such as if you want to link your Flare topics to source files and which style marks the beginning a each topic.

> ***Note*** — Import rules are stored in a Flare import file, which is saved in the Imports folder of the Project Organizer. For Word imports, the file's extension is .flimp; for FrameMaker imports, its extension is .flimpfm.

- Next, you'll **import the content** into your project, using the import rules.

Our recommendation

Before you import *all* your content files, we recommend that you set up the import file and try importing a small sample file first. Select a sample file that's somewhat representative of your other content files.

If you're not happy with the result, tweak the import settings in your Flare import file until you have all the settings the way you want them. There are many import settings and it might take a few test imports to decide exactly how you want to set it up.

> *Tip* — You can change a Flare import file from the **Project Organizer**. Simply open the **Imports** folder and double-click the name of the Flare import file you want to change.

Let's look more closely at some of the choices you'll make when you set up the import file.

DIVIDING ONE DOCUMENT INTO MANY TOPICS

As mentioned earlier, if a source file will be imported into more than one Flare topic, you must decide *where* you want to divide the source content.

A Word or FrameMaker document typically contains paragraphs of text separated by headings. Generally, Heading 1 is used for a major topic, and lower-level headings (Heading 2 or Heading 3) are used to divide sub-topics in the Heading 1 topic.

Before you import files, **choose a paragraph style (typically a heading style) at which to break topics**. Then **edit your document** to make sure that the content for each topic is preceded by the heading style you chose.

> *Note* — Multiple topics don't have to be contained in one physical source document. You can easily import multiple source files, even if each file contains content for only one topic.

An example

Suppose you chose the Heading 2 style as the dividing point between your topics. When you import your document, each unit of content between each Heading 2 style will be converted into a Flare topic, as shown in the following illustration.

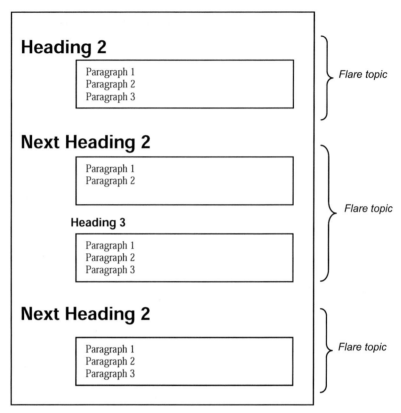

When you import this document, you'll end up with three Flare topics, as shown above.

CHOICES FOR IMPORTING STYLES

You should carefully consider the state of your documents' styles when deciding if you want to preserve them during import. Examine your source document(s) and ask:

- If you use local ("inline") formatting to control the appearance of your Word or FrameMaker files, do you want Flare to preserve that formatting?

- Are there lots of variations of styles? For example, do you have Heading 1, Heading 1 + bold, Heading 1 centered, Heading 1 underlined? Or are the styles clean (one type of Heading 1; one type of Heading 2, etc.)?

Then use this chart to help you decide the correct Flare import option.

Table B-2: *Choices for importing styles*	If ...	Use this import option ...
	You want to retain the styles in your source document *and* you don't have a proliferation of style variations - or - You want to retain the local formatting in your source document (Word files only)	**Preserve MS Word (or FrameMaker) Styles** With this option, Flare converts all Word or FrameMaker styles, including every style variation and custom style, to cascading stylesheet (CSS) styles.
	You want to use *only* the styles from a Flare stylesheet in your project	**Don't Preserve MS Word (or FrameMaker) Styles**

CHOICES FOR MAINTAINING CONTENT

Before you import your content, you'll need to decide where you will maintain it. You have two choices:

- **Option 1** — Use Flare to maintain your content after import. You will import your content just once and maintain it in Flare after that.

- **Option 2** — Use Word or FrameMaker to maintain your content after import. With this option, your Flare topics will be linked to the source files from which they were created, and **you will not change your topics in Flare.**

So how will Flare topics get updated if you choose Option 2? Time for more decisions ...

> **DECISION TIME!**
>
> If you choose Option 2, you will select one of these options:
>
> ✓ Have Flare check your source files and remind you when they have changed. It's then up to you to update your Flare topics by re-importing your Word or FrameMaker files.
>
> ✓ Have Flare check your source files for changes when you build the output, automatically re-import them, and update the corresponding Flare topics before building the output. This option is called **Easy Sync**.

Use this chart to help you decide on the right options for you.

Table B-3:
Options for
maintaining
content

Choose ...	When ...
Option 1: Maintain content in Flare	You don't need to keep the source files current. Changes are made by only one or two people (who have access to Flare).
Option 2: Maintain content in Word or FrameMaker	Some of the people editing content have Word or FrameMaker, but not Flare.
Easy Sync (available with Option 2)	You make frequent changes to your content. Changes are made by many people.

About Easy Sync

With Easy Sync, you don't have to guess if and when your content has changed. All changes to the source files will be incorporated before the Flare output is built.

> ***Important*** — When you use Easy Sync, don't change your topics in Flare! They will be lost with the next automatic re-import.

What if you change your mind after importing the content?

No problem! You can switch between linking your files and not linking them by using the Link Generate Files to Source Files checkbox on the Source Files tab in the Import Editor. If you unlink the source files, you must then begin updating your content with Flare instead of with Word or FrameMaker.

> *Tip* — You can also turn Easy Sync on and off for complete control over when changes are re-imported into Flare.

IMPORTING A WORD DOCUMENT

You can import Word documents in DOC, DOCX, or RTF (Rich Text) format that were created with Microsoft Word 2003 or 2007.

Flare can import the following items from Word files:

- text
- images
- formats
- index entries
- links
- cross-references

About Word drawing objects and images

Flare handles drawing objects and images in Word as follows:

- Flare puts imported images into your project's Resources folder, which is available in the Content Explorer.

- Flare does *not* import drawing objects, such as callouts, lines, and arrows.

- The text of floating text boxes can be imported, but the text will be anchored instead of floating.

If your Word file contains drawing objects, consider taking the actions listed on the following chart before you import your Word files.

Table B-4: *Actions to take before importing Word drawing objects*

If your Word file contains ...	Do this ...
Callouts and other drawing objects that annotate images	▪ Incorporate callouts into the image files before import *or* ▪ Use MadCap Capture to re-create the drawing objects. *Tip* — If you want to edit callouts after import, use Capture to create a graphics file that you can import. Because Capture stores graphic elements in layers, you can easily edit callouts later.
Drawings that do not annotate images	Import the drawings as raster or vector images in any of these formats: BMP, EMF, EXPS, GIF, HDP, JPG, JPEG, PNG, SWF, TIF, TIFF, WDP, WMF, XAML, or XPS.

How Flare creates TOCs from a Word document

Flare creates a new TOC from the topics you import. The TOC has the same name as the Word import file (your settings file).

However, if you created a TOC in Flare before importing your Word document, Flare does *not* add your imported topics to the existing TOC. To consolidate the new TOC with an existing one, simply link the new TOC to the existing TOC. Search on "linking a toc" in the Flare Help system for details.

How to import content from Word documents

Follow these instructions to import content from a Word document into a Flare project. This procedure includes instructions for creating the Word import file *and* importing the content.

🎀 To import content from a Word document:

1. Make sure that the Flare project to which you want to import content is open with the Project Organizer in view.

2. If you have previously imported Word documents into this project, skip to Step 3, next.

    If you have not previously imported Word documents into this project, you must create a Flare import file to store your import settings (rules for importing). Do the following:

    a. In the Project Organizer, right-click the **Imports** folder.

    b. Select **Add MS Word Import File** from the menu. The Add MS Word Import File dialog opens.

    c. To use a template provided with Flare, select **Factory Templates** in the Template Folder section and **MyWordImport** in the Templates section. To use one of your own templates, select **My Templates** for the folder and select the template you want to use from the list of templates on the right.

    > ***Important*** — You don't need to do anything with the Source File field, which Flare uses to store information about the import process for this and future imports.

d. Type a File Name. (Flare will add an extension of .flimp to the Word import file.)

e. Click **Add**, then **OK** to confirm the copy action. The File Name you typed is listed in the Imports folder and the Word Import Editor opens.

f. Skip to Step 5 below.

3. If you have previously imported documents into this project, expand the **Imports** folder.

4. Double-click the Flare import file you want to use for this import.

The Word Import Editor opens.

5. On the Source Files tab, do the following:

a. Click **Add Files** and select the Word documents you want to add. (You can choose DOC, DOCX, or RTF files.)

> **Note** — DOCX (Word's XML format) is available only with Word 2007.

b. If you want to update your content from Flare instead of from Word after import, clear the **Link Generated Files to**

Source Files checkbox. (See "Choices for maintaining content" on page 265 for options.)

c. If you've selected multiple Word documents to import, you can change the order in which they're listed by clicking **Move Up** and **Move Down**.

> ***Note*** — The document order shown here determines the topic order in the Flare TOC.

6. If you're splitting your documents into multiple topics, do the following:

   a. Click the **New Topic Styles** tab. On the left, Flare shows the styles used in the Word documents being imported.

   b. In the Used Word Styles column, double-click the style that will mark the beginning of each new topic. The style appears in the right column.

7. If you want Flare to incorporate changes from your linked Word documents each time you build your Flare output, do the following:

   a. Verify that the **Link Generated Files to Source Files** checkbox (Source Files tab) is checked.

   b. Click the **Options** tab, then check **Auto-reimport before 'Generate Output'**. (This feature is called "Easy Sync" in the Flare Help system.)

8. *(Optional)* On the Options tab, select these options if you have topics that are shorter than 50 characters, want to avoid creating empty topics, or want to split long topics in Word documents:

To ...	Use this option ...
Split long topics based on the number of characters (instead of using heading styles) and have Flare create a link called "Topic Continued" at the end of each page that is continued. You can also edit the link's format of the link.	Add "Topic Continued" links when appropriate

To ...	Use this option ...
Split long topics based on the number of characters and have Flare create a link called "Topic Continued From" at the top of each page that continues a split topic. You can also edit the format of the link.	Add "Topic Continued From" links when appropriate
Split long topics when a specified number of characters in the topic is reached. Enter the number of characters to use as a threshold. If a topic exceeds the threshold, it will be split.	Split Long Topics
Prevent Flare from creating topics for empty sections in your Word documents. Enter the threshold of empty characters. If a source topic exceeds the threshold, Flare will not create a topic for it.	Avoid Creating 'Empty' Topics

> **Important** — Clear this option if you have any topics that are shorter than 50 characters (the default threshold). If selected, Flare consolidates topics that are shorter than the threshold instead of creating separate topics. (Instead of clearing this option, you could also increase the threshold.)

To ...	Use this option ...
Specify a length for the file names Flare will create when it splits long topics.	Approximate Filename Length
Set imported tables to Auto-Fit to Contents so no table width is set.	Convert all tables to "Auto-Fit to Contents"

> **Note** — To learn more about these options, search for "creating topics" in the Flare Help system.

9. If you want the imported topics to be linked to a Flare stylesheet, click the **Stylesheet** tab and do the following:

   a. Select a stylesheet to apply to the imported Word topics. Either select Flare's standard stylesheet (Styles.css) or click the **Stylesheet** button and select the stylesheet already created for this project.

b. Select the appropriate button to either preserve or not preserve Word styles. (See "Choices for importing styles" on page 263.)

c. To create Flare styles for local formatting (not controlled by Word styles) in your Word document, check **Convert inline formatting to CSS styles**; otherwise, clear this option. (This option is available only if you preserve Word styles.)

> **Note** — In Word, you can apply formats by using toolbar buttons and menu options instead of character styles. In Flare, you'll hear the terms "local" formatting and "inline" formatting to describe this.

10. (*Optional*) If you want your Word *paragraph* styles to take on the characteristics of your Flare styles, map the styles by doing the following:

a. Click the **Paragraph Styles** tab.

b. For each Word style you want to map, select the style in the MS Word Style column, select a style (in the Flare Styles column) to map to it, then click **Map**. The Flare styles you select appear to the right of the Word styles you mapped them to, as shown here:

MS Word Style	Flare Style
Bodytext	p.Bodytext
Heading 1	h1.Heading 1
Heading 3	h3.Heading 3
Procedure	

Word style —— (points to Heading 3)

The Flare style it is mapped to. (In this example, we preserved Word styles.) —— (points to h3.Heading 3)

> **Note** — If you chose to preserve Word styles (on the Stylesheet tab), and you then map a Word style to a Flare style, Flare assigns each mapped style a new style name that is the combination of the two. For example, if the Word style is called "Heading 1" and the Flare style is called "h1," the resulting style after mapping is "h1.Heading 1." (The new style is a "style class" of the h1 style.)

Here's another example where we mapped paragraph styles but did *not* preserve Word styles. Notice how the resulting Flare style name is purely a Flare style name (h1), not a combination of the Word style (Heading 1) and the Flare style. (Flare did not create a new style.)

MS Word Style	Flare Style	
Bodytext	p	
Heading 1	h1	
Heading 2	h2	*The Flare style it is mapped to. (In this example, we did not preserve Word styles.)*

Word style ——

11. (*Optional*) If you want your Word *character* styles to take on the characteristics of your Flare styles, map the styles by doing the following:

   a. Click the **Character Styles** tab.

   b. For each Word style you want to map, select the style in the MS Word Style column, select a style in the Flare Styles column to map it to, then click **Map**.

12. Do one of the following:

   ▪ If you want to import the content now, proceed to Step 13, next.

   ▪ If you don't want to import the content now, click **Save All**, then close the Word Import Editor by clicking its close button (**x**).

13. Select **Import** (under the tab name). Then click **Yes** when prompted to save changes to the Flare import file.

   The Accept Imported Documents dialog opens, listing the documents to be imported (on the left) and a preview of the currently selected document (on the right).

14. If you're happy with how the topic previews look, click **Accept** to import the files. The files are added to your Flare project.

15. Close the Word Import Editor by clicking its close button (**x**).

Where are my imported topics?

You may notice that your imported topics aren't listed in the Content Explorer with your other project topics. That's because Flare put your imported topics together in a folder in the Content Explorer. That folder has the same name as the Word import file you created.

Figure B-1: *Where Flare stores your imported Word topics*

The folder that contains the imported topics has the same name as the Word import file.

If you have multiple import files, this is a handy way to keep track of which imported topics go to which import settings file.

IMPORTING A FRAMEMAKER DOCUMENT

You can import FrameMaker documents that were created with FrameMaker Versions 7.0 and newer in BOOK, FM, or MIF formats.

As already discussed, when you import a document, you can split it into multiple topics. Flare uses FrameMaker's heading styles as the division points.

Flare can import the following items from FrameMaker files:

- text

- images

- formats

- variables

- conditionals

- auto-numbering

- index entries

- hypertext links

- cross-references

Flare does *not* import FrameMaker master pages, so if you import a document that has master pages, you'll need to create Flare page layouts instead.

> **Best Practice** — If you have a FrameMaker book, it is better to import the book rather than individual files. Flare will identify and import the files that are part of the book.

About FrameMaker images

Flare handles images in FrameMaker as follows:

- Flare puts imported images in the same folder as imported topics. If you prefer, you can later move the images to the Resources\Images folder, which is the default folder for new images.

- Flare imports the text of anchored frames (such as text callouts) as an image.

- After import, you might need to resize or re-position images, since Flare does not anchor them in frames.

Before importing FrameMaker documents

When Flare imports your FrameMaker files, it uses the file name of the first FrameMaker source file as the file name of the first topic file it creates. If you want the file name to be the same as the text of the first heading, you must insert a marker in your first FrameMaker source file before you import the file.

> **Best Practice** — Insert a marker in every FrameMaker source file to be imported, not just the first one. (After all, you might later decide to rearrange the order in which you import the FrameMaker files.)

Add the marker at the *end* of the first heading in each FrameMaker file you want to import, not at the beginning of the heading. The marker should be a custom marker type called "Filename." For the text of the marker, type the file name for the first topic to be created from this source file. (For specific instructions, search the Flare Help system for "Specifying custom file names for FrameMaker imports.")

How to import content from FrameMaker documents

Follow these instructions to import content from a FrameMaker document into a Flare project. This procedure includes instructions for creating the FrameMaker import file *and* importing the content.

To import content from a FrameMaker document:

1. Make sure that the Flare project to which you want to import content is open with the Project Organizer in view.

2. If you have previously imported FrameMaker documents into this project, skip to Step 3, next.

   If you have not previously imported FrameMaker documents into this project, you must create a Flare import file to store your import settings (rules for importing). Do the following:

   a. In the Project Organizer, right-click the **Imports** folder.

b. Select **Add FrameMaker Import File** from the menu. The
Add FrameMaker Import File dialog opens.

c. To use a template provided with Flare, select **Factory
Templates** in the Template Folder section and
MyFrameImport in the Templates section. To use one of
your own templates, select **My Templates** for the folder and
select the template you want to use from the list of templates
on the right.

> *Important* — You don't need to do anything with the Source File
> field, which Flare uses to store information about the import process
> for this and future imports.

d. Type a File Name. (Flare will add an extension of .flimpfm to
the import file.)

e. Click **Add**, then click **OK** to confirm the copy action. The File
Name you typed is listed in the Imports folder and the
Frame Import Editor opens.

f. Skip to Step 5, below.

3. If you have previously imported documents into this project, expand the **Imports** folder.

4. Double-click the Flare import file you want to use for this import.

The Frame Import Editor opens.

5. On the **Source Files** tab, do the following:

a. Click **Add Files** and select the FrameMaker documents you want to add. (You can choose BOOK, FM, or MIF files.)

> ***Best Practice*** — If you're importing a FrameMaker book, it is better to import the book rather than individual FM files. Flare will identify and import the files that are part of the book.

b. If you want to update your content from Flare instead of from FrameMaker after import, clear the **Link Generated Files to Source Files** checkbox. (See "Choices for maintaining content" on page 265 for options.)

c. If you've selected multiple FrameMaker documents to import, you can change the order in which they're listed by clicking **Move Up** and **Move Down**.

> *Note* — The document order shown here determines the topic order in the Flare TOC.

6. If you're splitting your FrameMaker documents into multiple topics, do the following:

   a. Click the **New Topic Styles** tab. FrameMaker opens. Styles you use in the FrameMaker documents being imported are shown on the left.

   b. In the Used FrameMaker Styles column, double-click the style that will mark the beginning of each new topic. The style is listed in the right column.

7. (*Optional*) On the **Options** tab, select from among the following tasks:

To ...	Do this ...
Import the text contents of anchored frames (such as text callouts)	Check the **Generate Images for Anchored Frames when needed** box. The text will be imported as images. (Images contained in anchored frames will be imported as images whether or not you check this box.)
	Important — If you don't check this option, your text callouts will not be imported into Flare.
Incorporate changes in your linked FrameMaker documents each time you build Flare output	Verify that the **Link Generated Files to Source Files** box is checked (on the Source Files tab).
	Check the **Auto-reimport before 'Generate Output'** box. (This feature is called "Easy Sync" in the Flare Help system.)
Preserve the size of resized images in your FrameMaker documents	Check the **Preserve Image Size** box.

To ...	Do this ...
Enable passthrough markers (if used) in your FrameMaker documents	Check the **Enable 'Passthrough' Markers** box and select the format (text, fragment, or XML) of the passthrough markers. FrameMaker passthrough markers indicate text (such as JavaScript code) that requires special treatment when imported.
Create Flare table styles from the formats used in tables in your FrameMaker topics	Check the **Convert Table Styles** box. Table formatting will be imported even if you don't select this option.

8. (*Optional*) On the **Options** tab, select these options if you have topics that are shorter than 50 characters, want to avoid creating empty topics, or want to split long topics in FrameMaker documents:

To ...	Do this ...
Split long topics when a topic reaches a specified number of characters	Check the **Split Long Topics** box and enter the number of characters to use as a threshold. When a topic exceeds the threshold, it will be split.
Create a link called "Topic Continued" at the end of each Flare page that is continued	Check the **Add "Topic Continued" links when appropriate** box. You can also edit the format of the link.
Create a link called "Topic Continued From" at the top of each Flare page that continues a split topic	Check the **Add "Topic Continued From" links when appropriate** box. You can also edit the format of the link.

To ...	Do this ...
Prevent Flare from creating topics for empty sections in your FrameMaker documents	Check the **Avoid Creating 'Empty' Topics** box and enter the threshold of empty characters.
	When a source topic exceeds the threshold, Flare will not create a Flare topic for it.

> *Important* — Clear this option if you have any topics that are shorter than 50 characters (the default threshold). If selected, Flare consolidates topics that are shorter than the threshold instead of creating separate topics. (Instead of clearing this option, you could also increase the threshold.)

Specify a length for filenames Flare will create when it splits long topics.	Type a length in the **Approximate Filename Length** field.

> *Note* — To learn more about these options, search for "creating topics" in the Flare Help system.

9. On the **Stylesheet** tab, do the following:

    a. Select a stylesheet to apply to the imported FrameMaker topics. Either select Flare's standard stylesheet (Styles.css) or click the **Stylesheet** button and select the stylesheet already created for this project.

    b. Select the appropriate button to either preserve or not preserve FrameMaker styles. (See "Choices for importing styles" on page 263.)

    c. To specify the characteristics for each style's property group, click the **Conversion Styles** button to open the Import Styles Editor. Click the field to the right of each characteristic to select a value.

10. (*Optional*) If you want your FrameMaker *paragraph* styles to take on the characteristics of your Flare styles, map the styles by doing the following:

a. Click the **Paragraph Styles** tab.

b. For each FrameMaker style you want to map, select the style in the FrameMaker Style column, select a style (in the Flare Styles column) to map to it, then click **Map**. The Flare styles you select appear to the right of the FrameMaker styles you mapped them to, as shown here:

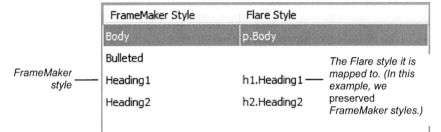

FrameMaker Style	Flare Style	
Body	p.Body	
Bulleted		*The Flare style it is*
Heading 1	h1.Heading 1	*mapped to. (In this example, we*
Heading 2	h2.Heading 2	*preserved FrameMaker styles.)*

FrameMaker style

> **Note** — If you chose to preserve FrameMaker styles (on the Stylesheet tab), and you then map a FrameMaker style to a Flare style, Flare assigns each mapped style a new style name that is the combination of the two. For example, if the FrameMaker style is called "Heading1" and the Flare style is called "h1," the resulting style after mapping is "h1.Heading1." (The new style is a "style class" of the h1 style.)

Here's another example where we mapped paragraph styles but did *not* preserve FrameMaker styles. Notice how the resulting Flare style name is purely a Flare style name (h1), not a combination of the FrameMaker style (Heading1) and the Flare style. (Flare did not create a new style.)

FrameMaker Style	Flare Style	
Body	p	
Bulleted		*The Flare style it is mapped*
Heading 1	h1	*to. (In this example, we did*
Heading 2	h2	*not preserve FrameMaker styles.)*

FrameMaker style

11. (*Optional*) To make your FrameMaker *character* styles take on the characteristics of your Flare styles, map the styles by doing the following:

    a.   Click the **Character Styles** tab.

    b.   For each FrameMaker style you want to map, select the style in the FrameMaker Style column, select a style in the Flare Styles column to map to it, then click **Map**.

12. (*Optional*) To make your FrameMaker *cross-references* take on the characteristics of a Flare style, map the styles by doing the following:

    a.   Click the **Cross References** tab.

    b.   For each FrameMaker style you want to map, select the style in the FrameMaker Style column, select a style in the Flare styles column to map to it, then click **Map**.

13. Do one of the following:

    ▪   If you want to import the content now, proceed to Step 14, next.

    ▪   If you don't want to import the content now, click **Save All** , then close the Word Import Editor by clicking its close button (**x**).

14. Select **Import** (under the tab name). Then click **Yes** when prompted to save changes to the Flare import file.

The Accept Imported Documents dialog opens and lists the documents to be imported (on the left) and a preview of the currently selected document (on the right).

15. If you're happy with how the topic previews look, click **Accept** to import the files. The files are added to your Flare project.

16. Close the FrameMaker Import Editor by clicking its close button (**x**).

Where are my imported topics and images?

You may have noticed that your imported topics aren't listed in the Content Explorer with your other project topics. That's because Flare put your imported topics together in a folder in the Content Explorer. This folder has the same name as the FrameMaker book file (if you imported a FrameMaker book) or as the first document listed at the top of the Source Files tab.

Flare placed your imported images in the same folder as the imported topics. (If you prefer, you can move the images to the Resources\Images folder, which is the default folder for new images.)

Figure B-2:
Where Flare stores your imported Frame-Maker topics

Imported topics

The folder that contains the imported topics has the same name as the FrameMaker import file.

If you have multiple import files, this is a handy way to keep track of which imported topics go to which import settings file.

IMPORTING HTML FILES

What if you have content that's in HTML format, such as website content? How can you get that content into a Flare project? It's quick and easy to do this with Flare.

Notes

Don't confuse HTML files and Flare files with an .htm extension. Flare files conform to the XML specification, HTML files do not.

If you copy an HTM file from another Flare project, it does not need to be converted.

When you import an HTML file, the style of your text looks the same as it did in your source HTML file.

Follow these instructions to import HTML files into a Flare project.

To import an HTML file:

1. Open Windows Explorer, select the HTML file(s) you want to import, and press **CTRL + C**.

2. In Windows Explorer, navigate to your Flare project folder and open its Content sub-folder.

3. Paste the files into the Content sub-folder (**CTRL + V**). The files are now available in Flare's Content Explorer.

4. Open the Content Explorer in Flare and double-click one of the HTML files you copied. Flare asks if you want to start the conversion process.

5. Click **Yes**. Flare shows you the contents of your original file and the converted one so you can be sure it looks okay before proceeding.

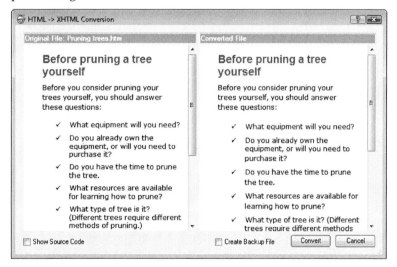

6. When you're ready to convert the file, click **Convert**. Flare converts the file to a topic and opens the topic in the XML Editor.

7. Repeat Steps 4 – 6 of this procedure for each file you copied into the project's Content folder.

Appendix C:
XML Editor
Reference

In this chapter ...

> Toolbars
> Cursor types
> Rulers
> Shortcuts when working with text
> Navigational shortcuts
> Apply color to text
> Use IntelliSense

TOP TOOLBAR

Click ...	To ...
Preview compiled topic	See how the topic will look when compiled. To learn more, see "Previewing a topic" on page 49.
F Open the Text Format toolbar	Open or close the Text Format toolbar, used to format the text in your topics.
Open the Review toolbar	Open or close the Review toolbar, used to send topics out for review, import a reviewed topic, insert annotations (comments), show annotations, and switch between edit and review mode.
Layout (Web) or Layout (Print) Layout Mode	Toggle between **Web Layout** and **Print Layout** modes. (See "Task 7: Viewing layout modes" on page 84.) Click the down arrow to select two additional choices: • **Edit Page Layout Document** — Opens the Page Layout Editor so you can edit the page layout associated with this topic. • **Edit Master Stylesheet** — Opens the Stylesheet Editor so you can edit the stylesheet associated with this topic (if there is one).
Medium: (default) Medium (default, non-print, print)	Select a medium to use when viewing your topic. (Flare uses the "default" medium for web layouts and the "print" medium for print layouts.) The XML Editor shows the topic in the styles associated with the medium you select. For more info, see "What are mediums?" on page 86.
Index Entry Mode	Toggle index entry mode on or off. Also contains a drop-down list of options for creating index keywords. To learn more about index entry mode, see "Adding index keywords" on page 171.
Insert a hyperlink	Open the Insert Hyperlink dialog box to add a hypertext link. Links can open topics within your project or external to your project, files, email addresses, websites, documents, or headings and bookmarks within the active topic.

Click ...	To ...
Insert a Cross-Reference	Open the Insert Cross-Reference dialog box to add a cross-reference to your topic. By default, the cross-reference inserts the word "See" plus the text of the block you are cross-referencing within quotes. You can create a cross-reference to a topic in the project, a file, a document, or a heading or bookmark within the active topic.
Insert a picture	Open the Insert Picture dialog box to insert a picture or graphics file. You can also type a screen tip that will appear when you hover your cursor over the picture.
Quick character ...	Select an ASCII character to insert. You can also enter the Unicode code for a symbol that you would like to be able to select with the Quick Character option.
Toggle show space	Toggle on or off the display of spaces and the end of block character ⤶ for the active topic.
Show tags	Toggle on or off the display of the *active* topic with its XML tags. (This is not editable code. If you want to edit a topic's code, you need to use a text editor such as Notepad or Flare's Internal Text Editor.) The drop-down list contains additional choices for various items such as variable names, bookmark names, and conditional indicators.

BOTTOM TOOLBAR

Click ...	To ...
Smaller Font (*Web Layout only*)	Lower the magnification of fonts in the *active* topic. Each time you click, the magnification is lowered by 10%. (You cannot reduce the magnification to below 100 %.) *Note* — This option does not reduce the size of images.

Click ...	To ...
[100] **Reset font scaling to 100%** (*Web Layout only*)	Reset the magnification of fonts in the *active* topic to 100%. (Does not change the font size.)
[+] **Larger Font** (*Web Layout only*)	Raise the magnification of fonts in the *active* topic. Each time you click, the magnification is raised by 10%.
[100% ▾] (*Web Layout only*)	Select a percentage by which to magnify the fonts in the *active* topic.
[◄◄] **Go to the first page** (*Print Layout only*)	Show the first page of the topic.
[◄] **Go to the previous page** (*Print Layout only*)	Show the previous page of the topic.
[►] **Go to the next page** (*Print Layout only*)	Show the next page of the topic.
[►►] **Go to the last page** (*Print Layout only*)	Show the last page of the topic.
[Page: 1 ▲▼ of 2] (*Print Layout only*)	Select the page number you want to view.
Zoom/scale (*Print Layout only*) **Note** — This button changes to reflect the current zoom/scale choice.	Specify how to magnify the page for the *active* topic: [100] **100 %** — Scales the content to 100% magnification. [□□] **100 % (2 pages)** — Shows two pages, each scaled to 100%. [↔] **Fit Width** — Scales the content to fit the window width.

Click ...	To ...
	☐ **One Page** — Scales the content to show one page.
	▥ **Two Pages** — Scales the content to show two pages.
	▦ **Four Pages** — Scales the content to show four pages.
	▦ **Eight Pages** — Scales the content to show eight pages.
Hide/show Conditional Indicators	Toggle on or off the highlighting of condition tags that have been applied to text in the *active* topic. See "Using condition tags" on page 328 for information about using condition tags in your topics.
Toggle show blocks	Toggle on or off tag bars in the *active* topic. Tag bars show the tag for each block in your topic.
	To learn more about tag bars, see page 89.
Toggle show spans	Toggle on or off span bars for the *active* topic.
	Span bars appear across the top of the content area and show the tags for formats applied to text. For example, if you apply bold to a word, a span bar labeled "b" appears above your topic.
	To learn more about span bars, see page 89.
Toggle show table rows	Toggle on or off table row (structure) bars in the *active* topic. (You must click inside a table to see its row bars.)
	There is one numbered bar for each row. You can resize or rearrange a table's rows by dragging its row bars.
	To learn more about table structure bars, see page 89.
Toggle show table columns	Toggle on or off column (structure) bars in the *active* topic. (You must click inside a table to see its column bars.)
	There is one bar for each column. The bars show the width of each column in pixels. You can resize or rearrange a table's columns by dragging its column bars.
	To learn more about table structure bars, see page 89.
Toggle show the horizontal ruler	Toggle on or off a horizontal ruler across the top of the *active* topic. Click the ruler to select the units of measure (pixels, points, centimeters, or inches) used.

Click ...	To ...
⊟ Toggle show the vertical ruler	Toggle on or off a vertical ruler at the left side of the *active* topic. Click the ruler to select the units of measure (pixels, points, centimeters, or inches) used.

Cursor types

There are other cursor shapes that we don't discuss here, but these are the most common ones. Refer to Figure C-1 when reading about cursor types.

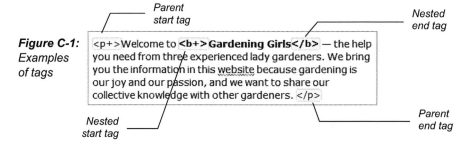

Figure C-1: Examples of tags

Cursor looks like this ...	When it's ...
[	Placed at a start tag.
	A start tag might be at the beginning of a text block or within a text block (an inline tag). For example, you might have applied bold to text within a text block. That text will be nested with its own tag set, as shown in Figure C-1.
]	Placed at an end tag.
I	Floating over text in a text block.
|	Anchored within a text block. (You clicked the mouse or used the keyboard to move the cursor in a text block.)
	When the cursor looks like this, you can edit text at the location of the cursor.

Cursor looks like this ...	When it's ...
|	Placed at the start of a nested tag.
	When the cursor looks like this, you can insert text in the parent tag after the nested end tag.
—	Placed between the end tag for a text block and the next start tag. For example, the cursor might be positioned after an end paragraph tag </p> and before the next start paragraph tag <p+>.
	When the cursor looks like this, you can insert text at the beginning of the next start tag.
	This cursor appears only when you use the keyboard (not the mouse) to navigate in your topic.
✛	Placed on the **Resize Picture** button at the lower right corner of an image. When the cursor looks like this, you can resize the image.
▷	Placed over a span bar (top structure bar).
	Click the structure bar to open a menu of choices that pertain to the text associated with the span bar.
🖑	Placed over the non-label area of a tag bar (left structure bar).
	Click the structure bar to open a menu of choices that pertain to the text block associated with the tag bar.
▷	Placed over the label of a tag bar (left structure bar).
	When the cursor looks like this, you can move the text block associated with the structure bar it is positioned over. Click, then drag and drop the bar to move the associated text.

> **Note** — The first seven cursors in this table appear only when you're not viewing tags (Reveal Tag mode).

RULERS

Rulers in the XML Editor work the same as in most word processing programs.

Figure C-2:
Horizontal and vertical rulers

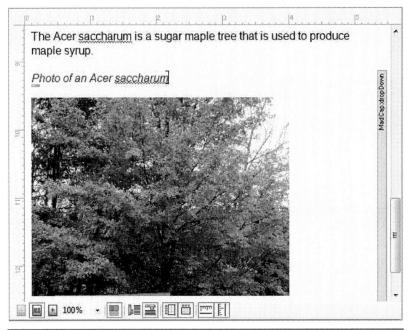

> *Note* — A ruler can be in view for one open topic, but not in view for another.

To show or hide the horizontal ruler:

- Click **Toggle Show the horizontal ruler** .

To show or hide the vertical ruler:

- Click **Toggle Show the vertical ruler** .

To change a ruler's units of measure:

1. Click the ruler.

2. Select the units of measure you want (pixels, points, centimeters, inches).

SHORTCUTS WHEN WORKING WITH TEXT

SELECTING TEXT

To select ...	Do this ...
A word	Double-click the word
A block of text	Triple-click anywhere within the text block
	- or -
	Hover your cursor over the non-label portion of the block's tag bar and click the bar when the cursor changes to a
	hand. Select **Select** from the context menu.
The entire topic	Select **Edit → Select All**
	- or -
	Click four times in fast succession.

DELETING TEXT

To ...	Do this ...
Delete the character to the right of the insertion point	Press **DELETE**.

To ...	Do this ...
Delete the character to the left of the insertion point	Press **BACKSPACE**.
Delete several consecutive words	Select the words. Then press **DELETE**, select **Edit →** **Delete**, or click the **Delete** ☒ button.
Delete an entire text block	Select the text block and press **DELETE** - or - Hover your cursor over the block's structure tag. When the cursor changes to a hand 🖑, select the structure tag, then select **Edit → Delete** from the structure menu. *Note* — The start and end tags for the text block are also deleted.

COPYING AND PASTING TEXT

You can copy (**CTRL + C**) and paste (**CTRL + V**) text as you would in most word processing applications, but you can also use the tag hint bar to open a context menu that contains copy and paste options. (For more info, see "Copying and pasting text into a topic" on page 98 and "Using tag hint bars and context menus" on page 93.)

MOVING TEXT WITHIN A TOPIC

Use the following procedures to move a word, several consecutive words, or entire blocks of text.

To move a one word or several consecutive words:

1. Select the words to be moved. (See the chart on page 297 for assistance.)

2. Cut the selected text (**CTRL + X**) and paste it (**CTRL + V**) where desired within the topic.

To move a text block:

Do one of the following:

- Select the text block to be moved. (See the chart on page 297 for assistance.) Cut the text block (**CTRL + X**) and paste it (**CTRL + V**) where desired within the topic.

- Make sure that tag bars are in view. (If not, click the **Toggle show blocks** button.) Then do one of the following:

  - Drag and drop the text block's tag bar to the desired place in the topic.

  - Hover your cursor over the text block's tag bar until the cursor changes to a hand, then click the structure bar and select **Move Up** or **Move Down**.

Note — To learn more about tag bars, see "Toggling tag and span bars" on page 91.

NAVIGATIONAL SHORTCUTS

To move to ...	Do this ...
The top of the topic	Press **CTRL + HOME**. A blinking left bracket [appears before the first word in the block.
The end of the topic	Press **CTRL + END**. A blinking right bracket] appears after the last word in the block.
The next page of print output (*in Print Output mode*)	Press **PAGE DOWN**.
The previous page of print output (*in Print Output mode*)	Press **PAGE UP**.
The end of the block of text your cursor is in	Press **END**. A blinking right bracket] appears after the last word in the block.

To move to ...	Do this ...
The end of the current paragraph	Press **ENTER**. This option also starts a new paragraph.
The next word	**CTRL + →**
The previous word	**CTRL + ←**

APPLYING COLOR TO TEXT

 To apply a color to text:

1. Select the text.

2. Select **Format → Color**.

3. Choose a color from the color chart.

USING INTELLISENSE

IntelliSense is an XML Editor feature that predicts ways to complete the word or phrase you are typing. As you type, IntelliSense displays a popup that shows words and phrases you've already used (matching phrases). If you see the word or phrase you want inserted, you can quickly select it, thus saving you typing time.

You can also view and select these things:

- **variables** contained in the open project

- **frequent phrases** (phrases you've used frequently in the open project)

Lists words and phrases from your project that match what you are typing.

Lists frequently used words and phrases from your project.

Figure C-3: IntelliSense popup

Changes IntelliSense properties.

Lists variables used in this project.

CHANGING INTELLISENSE SETTINGS

By changing IntelliSense settings, you can change the results that appear in the IntelliSense popup for matching and frequent phrases. For example, you can set minimums and maximum for the number of words that should appear in the popup, and you can set a value for the number of times a phrase should occur to be considered frequent.

IntelliSense is preset with defaults for these settings. If those don't meet your needs, you can learn more by searching for "IntelliSense dialog" in the Flare Help system.

Note — To use IntelliSense, Microsoft SQL Server must be installed.

Once the IntelliSense popup appears, here's what you can do.

To select a suggestion:

1. (*Optional*) Select the IntelliSense button for frequent phrases or project variables.

2. To insert a word, phrase, or variable, do one of the following:

   - Double-click the row.

   - Click the row once and press **ENTER**.

To dismiss the popup:

To ignore the IntelliSense suggestions and dismiss the popup, do one of the following:

- Keep typing the word.

- Click the IntelliSense close button (**x**).

If you find yourself dismissing the popup often, try changing the IntelliSense settings. If you decide that IntelliSense is not helpful for your project, you can disable it.

DISABLING AND ENABLING INTELLISENSE

IntelliSense is enabled by default, but can be easily disabled by clicking the **Disable IntelliSense** Disable IntelliSense button on the IntelliSense popup.

> *Note* — To re-enable IntelliSense, select **Edit → IntelliSense → Enable IntelliSense**.

Appendix D: Context- Sensitive Help

In this chapter …

➤ Learn about context-sensitive help
➤ Create a header file
➤ Create an alias file
➤ Set up an alias file
➤ Test your context-sensitive help

Overview

This appendix pertains to Help systems only. Further, it applies only if the application you are writing Help for will have help buttons on its windows and dialogs.

Creating context-sensitive help is a collaboration between you (the help author) and the software developers of the application you are writing Help for. When you develop context-sensitive help, you'll work closely with software developers to make it happen.

What is context-sensitive help?

Context-sensitive help links an application's window or dialog to a help topic that explains it. Users can access a help topic by clicking a help button or pressing **F1** from the associated window or dialog.

With context-sensitive help, a software developer places help buttons on the windows and dialogs where Help is needed. As the help author, you'll write the help topics that the help buttons will open—plus you'll indicate ahead of time which topics go with which dialogs. This process is called **mapping**, and it uses two kinds of files:

- Header file
- Alias file

HEADER FILE

Header files (also called map files) assign a unique identification number (map number) to each window and dialog that will open a help topic. The choice of which windows and dialogs will have context-sensitive help is a decision you and the software developers will make and depends on the content of your Help system.

Header files are text files, readable in Notepad. They have an extension of .h or .hh, which is added automatically by Flare.

Software developers may provide the header file, but if not, you can use Flare to create it, and then add topic IDs used by an application and map numbers to it. If you create the header file, you'll need to discuss with the software developers what it should contain, because the map numbers must match the topic IDs used in the application. For more information about this, see "Creating a header file" on page 308.

Here's an example of a header file. (Header files typically have more than five lines, but for the sake of space, we show just five here.)

Figure D-1:
Header file

ALIAS FILE

An alias file is used to assign each map number to a topic in your Flare Help project. You'll create alias files from Flare in a format readable only by Flare (you cannot view them in Notepad). Alias files have an .flali extension.

In addition to assigning windows and dialogs to help topics, you can also assign a **skin** to each help topic so you can change the appearance of the context-sensitive help. For example, you might want context-sensitive topics to open in a smaller window than your regular help topics.

Think of an alias file as the "go-between" that connects a software application and your Help system.

AN EXAMPLE OF MAPPING

Suppose that your application contains an Add dialog, a Change dialog, and a Properties dialog, each of which need to open context-sensitive help. In addition, assume that ...

Table D-1:
Example
of mapping

This dialog's help button ...	Should open this topic ...
Add dialog	Adding a widget
Change dialog	Changing a widget
Properties dialog	Widget properties

The header and alias files in our example would contain:

```
Header file

Add_acct_dialog        1
Change_acct_dialog     2
Properties_dialog      3
```

```
Alias file

Add_acct_dialog        1    Adding a widget
Change_acct_dialog     2    Changing a widget
Properties_dialog      3    Widget properties
```

HOW FLARE USES CONTEXT-SENSITIVE HELP

Let's look at how Flare uses help buttons to open Flare help topics:

Flare uses this button to open a topic that
contains information about this dialog.

Figure D-2:
Help
buttons on
a dialog

Flare uses this button to open a topic that contains
information about this part of the dialog.

YOUR TASKS

To create context-sensitive help in Flare, you'll need to complete these tasks:

- **Planning.** Talk to the software developer and decide which windows and dialogs require context-sensitive help and whether context-sensitive help topics will open in windows that are sized or positioned differently than regular help topics.

- Verify that your **project contains a header file**.

  If the software developer gives you a header file, you must import it into your project. (You can find instructions for importing a header file in the Flare Help system by searching on "header files" and opening the topic called "Importing Header Files.") Alternately, you can copy the header file into the Project Organizer's Advanced folder (<project name>\project\advanced).

  If the software developer doesn't give you a header file, create a header file in Flare. See "Creating a header file" next.

- **Add an alias file** to your project. See "Adding an alias file" on page 310.

- **Set up the alias file.** This involves creating topic IDs and map numbers (only if you didn't' get a header file from the software developer), mapping topic IDs to help topics, and optionally assigning a skin to topic IDs. See "Setting up an alias file" on page 311.

- **Select the alias file when you set up the target.** To do this, open the target in the Target Editor, click the **Advanced** tab, and select the alias file.

- *If you create the header file*, **give it to the software developer.** (For instructions, search on "header files" in the Flare Help system and open the topic called "Providing a Developer with a Header File.")

- **Test the context-sensitive help links** using Flare.

- **Build the output** and **give output files to the software developers**.

CREATING A HEADER FILE

If you do not get a header file from the software developer, you'll need to create one. This requires two steps:

- (*Optional*) **Add a header file to your project**. Skip this step if you already have a header file in the Advanced folder of the Project Organizer.

   Flare creates a default header file when you create a new project. If you want to use that header file, you don't need to add another one to your project.

Figure D-3:
Default
header file

Default header file

The default header file contains one line:

Figure D-4:
Contents of
the default
header file

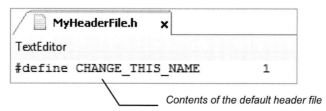

Contents of the default header file

- **Add content to the header file**—This involves creating one line for each window or dialog that will link to a help topic. Each line contains a topic ID (such as add_acct_dialog) and a unique map number. *You'll add content to the header file when you set up the alias file.*

ADDING A HEADER FILE TO YOUR PROJECT

If you don't want to use the default header file, complete the following procedure to add a new header file.

To add a header file to your project:

1. Select **Project → Advanced → Add Header File**. The Add Header File dialog opens.

2. Select a template folder and template.

3. Type a File Name for the header file.

4. Click **Add**, then **OK** to copy the header file to the project.

   The header file is copied to your project in the Project Organizer's Advanced folder.

ADDING CONTENT TO THE HEADER FILE

Adding content means adding a line for each window or dialog that will open a help topic. Each window or dialog will be a separate line, and each line will contain a **topic ID** and a unique **map number** for that window or dialog as show in Figure D-1.

Flare automatically adds content (topic IDs and map numbers) to the header file when you assign help topics to windows and dialogs in the Alias Editor, as described next.

ADDING AN ALIAS FILE

Before adding an alias file, make sure that your project already has a header file (see the previous topic).

To add an alias file to your project:

1. Select **Project** → **Advanced** → **Add Alias File**. The Add Alias File dialog opens.

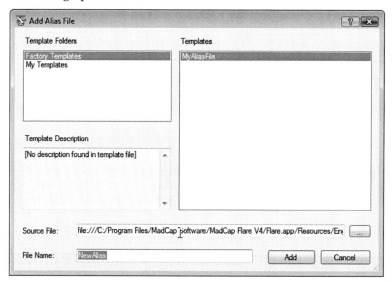

2. Select a template folder and a template.

3. Type a File Name for the alias file.

4. Click **Add**, then **OK** to copy the alias file to the project.

   The alias file opens in the Alias Editor and is copied to your project in the Project Organizer's Advanced folder.

Note — You can set up the alias file now or later.

5. If you don't want to set up the alias file now, close the Alias
    Editor (**x**).

SETTING UP AN ALIAS FILE

Setting up an alias file involves these tasks:

- (*If you created the header file*) **Creating topic IDs and unique map
  numbers**. You don't need to complete this task if you received a
  header file from a software developer.

- **Mapping.** This involves assigning help topics to windows and
  dialogs, which simultaneously creates the topic IDs and map
  numbers in the header file.

- (*Optional*) **Assigning a skin to topic IDs**.

Use the following procedure to set up an alias file.

To set up an alias file:

1. If the alias file is not open in the Alias Editor, open it now by
   double-clicking it in the Advanced folder of the Project
   Organizer.

*An identifier is
another name for
a topic ID.*

The left side of the Alias Editor lists the contents of your header
files: identifier (topic ID) and value. It also has places for you to
assign a topic and a skin to this identifier. If you have more than
one header file, it lists the identifiers from all of them.

2. If you have more than one header file, click the down arrow to
   the right of "all identifiers" and select the appropriate header file
   from the list.

> ***Note*** — If you received a header file from the software developer, the left
> side of the Alias Editor will contain many lines (one for each topic ID/map
> number combination). Otherwise, the left side will show only what's in the
> header file you created ("CHANGE_THIS_NAME" if it's a new header file
> that you've done nothing with).

New and default header files contain a placeholder identifier
("CHANGE_THIS_NAME").

Identifier	Topic	Value	Skin	Header File
CHANGE_THIS_...		1		MyHeaderFile.h

3. Complete the tasks listed in the following chart as applicable.

To ...	Do this ...
Change the text of an identifier	▪ Click the identifier. ▪ Type the new name. (Use underscores instead of spaces to separate the words.) **Identifier / Topic / Value / Skin / Header File** ADD_ACCT_DIA... / / 1 / / MyHeaderFile.h
Create a new identifier (a new row)	▪ Click **New Identifier**. A new row appears on the left with an assigned value and a temporary name (NEW1). **Identifier / Topic / Value / Skin / Header File** ADD_ACCT_DIA... / Adding an ... / 1 / CSH ... / MyHeaderFile.h NEW1 / / 1000 / / MyHeaderFile.h
Change the value	▪ Click the value and type the new value.
Delete an identifier	▪ Select the identifier and click **Remove**.
Map a topic to an identifier listed on the left	▪ Select the identifier. ▪ Select a topic (from the right) to map to the identifier. ▪ Click **Assign**. **Identifier / Topic / Value / Skin / Header File** ADD_ACCT_DIA... / Adding an ... / 1 / / MyHeaderFile.h
Map a skin to an identifier listed on the left	▪ Select the identifier. ▪ Select a skin (bottom right) to map to the identifier. ▪ Click Assign Skin. **Identifier / Topic / Value / Skin / Header File** ADD_ACCT_DIA... / Adding an ... / 1 / CSH ... / MyHeaderFile.h

4. To create a new identifier and map a topic to it:

   a. Select a topic (from the right) to map to the identifier.

   b. Click **Assign New**. The Assign New Identifier dialog opens.

   c. Type the new identifier name. (Use underscores instead of spaces to separate the words.)

   d. Type a value.

   e. Click **OK**.

     The identifier appears on the left and is mapped to the topic that you selected.

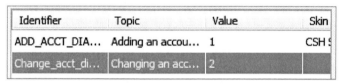

5. When you're done creating identifiers and mapping topics, click **Save All** 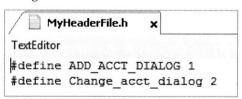 to save the changes you made to the alias and header files.

Notice that Flare automatically updates the header file when you change the alias file.

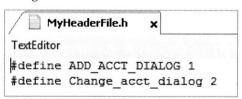

TESTING YOUR CONTEXT-SENSITIVE HELP

It's a good idea to test your context-sensitive help links in two ways:

- **From the software application** after you've built your Help system and given it to the software developer to link into the application. Click the help button from each window or dialog that is linked to a help topic.

- **From Flare** (discussed next).

TESTING CONTEXT-SENSITIVE HELP FROM FLARE

Use the following procedure to test context-sensitive links after you have mapped topics to identifiers and built the Help.

To test your help links from Flare:

1. Build the output for the Help system (see Step 5B: Create Online Output).

2. Right-click the Help target and select **Test CSH API Calls <target name>** from the menu.

   The Context Sensitive Help (CSH) API Tester dialog appears.

3. For each Topic Identifier, click ⎡Test⎤. The help topic linked to
    the identifier opens in a separate window. If the correct topic
    does not appear, you'll need to check its mapping in the alias
    file.

    If you see the message "found no topic identifiers in target,"
    check to make sure that the alias file is set up and that you
    selected it on the Advanced tab of the Target Editor for your
    Help target.

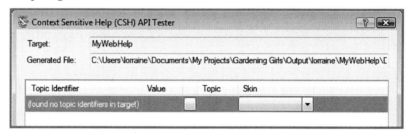

4. When you are done testing links, click **Close**.

Appendix E: Troubleshoot

In this chapter …

> Broken links
> Unlinked TOC items
> Image issues with Internet Explorer
> Build errors
> Analyzer

OVERVIEW

Here are some common problems that can occur in your projects:

- Broken links

- Broken bookmark links

- Build errors

- Unlinked TOC items

- Unlinked TOC books. (This is not a problem if you choose not to link TOC books by design.)

> **Note** — Don't confuse unlinked items with broken links. A *broken link* is one that no longer works because the file or path to it is no longer valid. An *unlinked TOC item* is not linked to anything.

Here's another, less common problem that we've experienced:

- Images that don't show up in WebHelp output viewed with Internet Explorer

Continue reading to find out why these problems occur and how to fix them.

BROKEN LINKS AND UNLINKED ITEMS

Flare attempts to help you avoid broken links. For example, if you try to delete a file (topic, image, page layout, master page, stylesheet or skin, for example) that something else links to, Flare lets you know and asks how you want to handle the links.

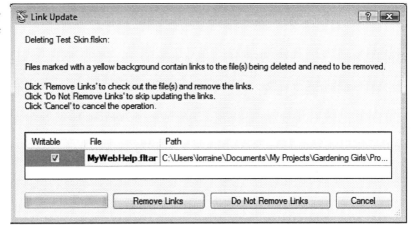

Figure E-1:
Flare warns you when you try to delete files that are linked

However, you can still end up with broken links in your project. Here are some reasons why.

POSSIBLE CAUSES

Broken links sometimes occur if you:

- Change a topic's file name

- Move a linked topic file to a different folder in the Content Explorer

- Delete a file that was linked to another file (topic, table of contents, or target, for example), and you selected **Do Not Remove Links** when prompted

HOW BROKEN LINKS AND UNLINKED ITEMS APPEAR IN THE TOC

The TOC Editor marks broken links and unlinked items and books with red symbols.

Figure E-2:
Broken links
and unlinked
items in a
TOC

Viewing a summary of TOC issues

To view a summary of broken links and unlinked items, click

 in the TOC Editor toolbar.

The dialog in Figure E-3 shows current issues in the TOC visible in the TOC Editor. (Unlinked books are not necessarily a problem. You might intentionally have not linked TOC books to topics.)

Figure E-3:
TOC dialog
showing the
number of
broken and
unlinked
items

UNLINKED TOC ITEMS

You'll end up with *unlinked TOC items* if you add a new TOC item by clicking **New item** in the TOC Editor toolbar and then forget to link the TOC item to a topic.

> *Best Practice* — To avoid unlinked TOC items, create a TOC item and topic simultaneously by clicking **Create a new topic and link to it** 🖼 in the TOC Editor toolbar.

🎓 To fix an unlinked TOC item:

1. Open the Content Explorer.

2. Drag and drop a topic from the Content Explorer to the applicable item in the TOC Editor.

   The item is linked and the unlinked symbol ⚒ disappears.

PROBLEMS WITH IMAGES

It's typical to add images (photographs, screen captures, and illustrations) to topics. Flare supports these image formats: BMP, EMF, EXPS, GIF, HDP, JPG, PNG, SWF, TIF, TIFF, WDP, WMF, XAML, and XPS.

However, be careful when converting an image from one format to another before you insert it into a Flare topic. You can easily corrupt an image file without even knowing it.

If one or more of your images don't appear when you view WebHelp output with Internet Explorer, it's likely that you have one or more corrupt images in your project. It's our experience that if you insert a corrupt image into your Flare project, Internet Explorer may display the image sometimes, and sometimes not!

It can be very difficult to determine which image is the culprit because all images appear normal when viewed in the XML Editor. But here's a clue: **If Windows Explorer encounters a corrupt image, all images after that disappear.** Firefox, however, seems unaffected by the same images and displays all output as expected.

Build errors

When Flare builds your output, it checks for errors. If it finds any, the following message appears:

Figure E-4:
Build error

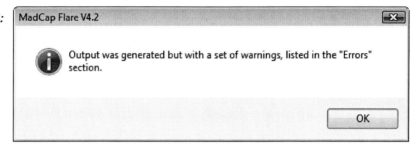

Click the **Errors** tab to view the errors.

Topic that contains the
bad link

Figure E-5: *Build Progress Errors tab*

File the topic links to

You can also click **Save Log** to save these messages in an error report. Then click **OK** to confirm that the log was saved in the Project Organizer's Reports folder.

> ***Best Practice*** — Save errors in a log so you can keep it open while fixing topics. (You cannot open topics to fix errors until you close this dialog.)

OPENING THE ERROR LOG FILE

Use the following procedure to open an error log that you saved after building output.

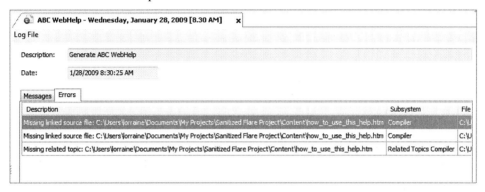 To open the error log:

1. In the Project Organizer, expand the **Reports** folder and double-click the log file you previously saved. The log file opens in the middle pane.

ABC WebHelp - Wednesday, January 28, 2009 [8.30 AM] ×		
Log File		
Description:	Generate ABC WebHelp	
Date:	1/28/2009 8:30:25 AM	

Messages | **Errors**

Description	Subsystem	File
Missing linked source file: C:\Users\lorraine\Documents\My Projects\Sanitized Flare Project\Content\how_to_use_this_help.htm	Compiler	C:\U
Missing linked source file: C:\Users\lorraine\Documents\My Projects\Sanitized Flare Project\Content\how_to_use_this_help.htm	Compiler	C:\U
Missing related topic: C:\Users\lorraine\Documents\My Projects\Sanitized Flare Project\Content\how_to_use_this_help.htm	Related Topics Compiler	C:\U

2. Scroll to the right (if necessary) to view the file that contains the bad link (in the "File" column).

3. Double-click the row in the error log that lists the file with the bad link. Fix the link, using this chart as a guide.

If the problem is a ...	Do this ...
Missing linked source file in a TOC	<ul><li>Right-click the TOC item.</li><li>Select **Link to Topic.**</li><li>Select the topic to link to.</li><li>Save the TOC.</li></ul>
Missing related topic	<ul><li>Right-click the **Related Topics** Help control.</li><li>Select **Edit Related Topics Control**.</li><li>On the right side of the Insert Related Topics Control dialog, select the correct file to link to.</li><li>Click **OK**. Save the topic.</li></ul>

If the problem is a ...	Do this ...
Missing linked source file in a topic	<ul><li>Right-click the bad link.</li><li>Select **Edit Hyperlink.**</li><li>On the Insert Hyperlink dialog, reselect the topic (file, document, etc.) to link to.</li><li>Save the topic.</li></ul>

To analyze your project for errors *before* building output, read the next section.

ANALYZING YOUR PROJECT

Flare offers two analyzers that help diagnose problems in your projects:

- **Internal analyzer** (provided with Flare)

- **External analyzer** (MadCap Analyzer, purchased separately)

This section discusses the internal analyzer.

WHAT YOU CAN ANALYZE

With the internal analyzer, you can examine your Flare project for the following problems:

- Broken links

- Topics that aren't linked to a TOC (to a TOC you select or to any TOC in your project)

- Topics that do not contain any index markers

- Incoming links (links that point to the current file from other files)

- Project annotations (a list of files that have annotations)

- Database errors (project files that are not scanned for errors because they are incompatible with the analyzer)

> *Important* — If your project has database errors, submit a bug report to MadCap Software Technical Support. To do so, click **Feature Requests** at the bottom of the Start Page.

ANALYZING YOUR PROJECT

Use the following procedure to analyze your project with Flare's internal analyzer.

To analyze your project:

1. Select **View** → **Project Analysis**. The Project Analysis window opens in the left pane.

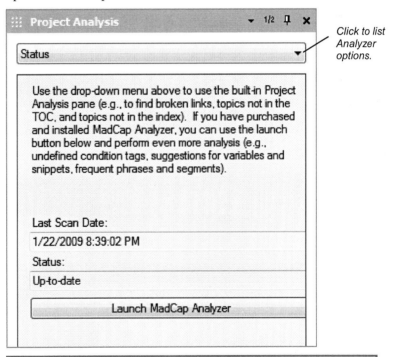

Click to list Analyzer options.

> *Tip* — Expand the left pane to see more of the Project Analysis window.

2. Select an option from the list.

To ...	Select this from the list ...
See when your project was last analyzed	**Status**
Check your project for broken links and bookmarks	**Broken links**
See which topics have not been linked to a TOC	**Topics not in selected TOC** Then select the TOC from the Filter list.
See which topics don't have index entries	**Topics not in Index** Then select the TOC from the list.
View a list of files that point to the file that is active in the middle pane	**Incoming Links** Then click Browse Links .
View a list of files that contain annotations	**Project Annotations**
View a list of files with database problems	**Database Errors**

3. (*Optional*) Double-click a file to open its topic.

4. To open MadCap Analyzer (a separate software product), select **Status** from the list and click **Launch MadCap Analyzer**. Analyzer opens in a new window.

> **Note** — This book describes how to analyze a project with Flare's internal analyzer. It does not cover MadCap Analyzer.

5. When you're done analyzing your project, close the Project Analysis window (**x**).

Appendix F:
Single-
Sourcing

In this chapter …

> Flare features for single-sourcing
> Use condition tags
> Create and changing snippets
> Add variables

OVERVIEW

Single-sourcing can be summarized in one phrase: **Create once, use many!** With Flare, you create content once and reuse it in any number of topics and outputs.

Flare provides these features for single-sourcing your content:

- **Condition tags**, which mark content for a particular target.

- **Snippets**, which are small units of content you reuse in multiple topics.

- **Variables**, which store changeable content (such as customer names and version numbers) that you can use in multiple topics. When you build your output, Flare substitutes the variable value everywhere it is used.

- **Multiple targets** from the same content (commonly called "multi-channel publishing"). Targets are described in the Document Basics chapter, Step 5A: Create Print Output, and Step 5B: Create Online Output.

Read the rest of this chapter to find out how to use condition tags, snippets and variables in your Flare project.

USING CONDITION TAGS

A condition tag is a marker you apply to content so that content shows up in some of your outputs but not in others.

Condition tags let you create output that contains variations of a project's content. In a *single* project, you can store the common content and the variations of it. No need to spend the time and money creating different documents that duplicate common content for different needs.

With condition tags, you tag only the variations of content, not the common content that is reused for all outputs. When you set up your target, you specify which condition tags to include or exclude for that target.

> *Note* — You can apply condition tags to topics, images, stylesheets, full paragraphs, text within paragraphs, table rows and columns, TOC entries, and index keyword markers.

AN EXAMPLE

Suppose you need to create two Help systems, one for an insurance program in NY and another for an insurance program in CA. Here's what you'd do:

1. Create all the content for both Help systems in one project (instead of two separate projects).

2. Create one condition tag called "Insurance NY" and another called "Insurance CA."

3. Apply the "Insurance NY" condition tag to the content that belongs only in the Help system for NY insurance users.

4. Apply the "Insurance CA" condition tag to the content that belongs only in the Help system for CA insurance users.

5. Create two targets: one for Insurance NY and one for Insurance CA.

6. Set up the Insurance NY target to include the Insurance NY condition tag and exclude the Insurance CA tag.

7. Set up the Insurance CA target to include the Insurance CA condition tag and exclude the Insurance NY tag.

TERMS YOU SHOULD KNOW

Before you continue, let's clarify the difference between a couple of Flare terms:

- **Condition tag set** — A named group of condition tags. Condition tag sets are listed in the Project Organizer's Conditional Text folder. You can create as many sets as you want.

> *Note* — To create a condition tag set, select **Project → Add Condition Tag Set**.

- **Condition tag** — A color-coded marker that you apply to content. Condition tags are contained in a condition tag set. You can create multiple tags in a single set.

CREATING CONDITION TAGS

Use the following procedure to add or change a condition tag (not a condition tag set).

To create a condition tag:

1. Open the Project Organizer.

2. Expand the **Conditional Text** folder, which shows existing condition tag sets. Flare includes a default condition tag set.

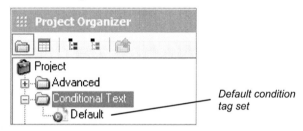

Default condition tag set

3. Double-click the condition tag set you want to add tags to. The Condition TagSet Editor opens, showing existing tags for the tag set.

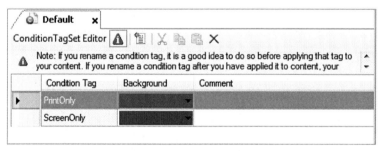

The default condition tag set contains two condition tags: "PrintOnly" and "ScreenOnly." Each condition tag has a unique color that highlights the content tagged with it.

4. Add or change tags as described in this table:

To ...	Do this ...
Add a new tag	▪ In the Condition TagSet Editor's toolbar, click **New item** . A new row appears. ▪ To change the tag name, click it, press **F2**, and type a new name.
Rename a tag	▪ Click the tag name and press **F2**. ▪ Type a new name for the tag.
Change a tag's color	▪ Click the Background drop-down arrow and select **Pick Color**. The Color Picker dialog opens. ▪ Select a color and click **OK**. (Only you will see the color; it doesn't appear in the output.)
Add comments to a tag	▪ Click in the tag's **Comment** field. ▪ Press **F2** and type the comment. (Comments don't appear in the output.)

5. When you're done adding or changing tags, click **Save All** to save your work.

After creating condition tags, you can apply them to your content.

APPLYING CONDITION TAGS

Flare provides two ways to apply a condition tag to text in the XML Editor. You can apply a condition tag to:

▪   Only the text you select

▪   An entire text block

If **Hide/show Conditional Indicators** is selected on the XML Editor's bottom toolbar, the text that is marked with a condition tag is highlighted in color. Each condition tag is assigned a unique color.

> **Note** — Before you can apply a condition tag, you must create it. See the previous topic.

To apply a condition tag to selected text:

1. Select the text you want to apply the condition tag to.

2. Select **Format → Conditions**. The Condition Tags dialog opens.

3. Select the condition tag set that contains the condition tag you want to apply.

4. Check the checkbox for the condition tag you want to apply, and click **OK**.

    Flare applies the condition tag to the selected text. If **Hide/show Conditional Indicators** is turned on, the text is highlighted with the condition tag's color.

    > o share our collective knowledge with other gard
    > or designs, and maybe help you with your garde
    > y. This text is encoded with a condition tag.

    If span bars are visible, they show that text has been tagged with a condition tag. (Span bars appear above the content area.)

Span bar

Tip — To turn on span bars, click **Toggle show spans** on the XML Editor's bottom toolbar.

To apply a condition tag to an entire text block:

1. If not in view, show the tag structure bars on the XML Editor's bottom toolbar.

2. Place your cursor anywhere in the text block where you want to apply the condition tag.

3. Hover your cursor over the text block's structure bar until the cursor changes to a hand. Then click the structure bar to open a popup menu.

4. From the popup menu, select **Conditions**. The Condition Tags dialog appears.

5. Select the **Condition Tag Set** that contains the condition tag you want to apply.

6. Check the checkbox for the **Condition Tag** you want to apply, and click **OK**.

    Flare applies the condition tag to the entire text block and highlights its structure bar with that condition tag's color. If **Hide/show Conditional Indicators** ▓ is turned on, the text block is also highlighted with the condition tag's color.

Condition tag applied to selected text.

Condition tag applied to text block

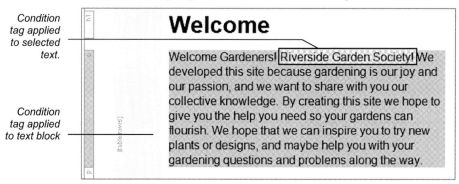

To highlight text tagged with condition tags:

1. If not in view, show the tag structure bars ▤ on the XML Editor's bottom toolbar.

2. Select the text you want to apply the condition tag to.

USING SNIPPETS

Snippets are units of content that you create when you need to include the same content in more than one topic. They're a perfect example of reusing content.

The beauty of snippets is maintenance. You change *only* the snippet; Flare updates it everywhere the snippet is used. Done!

Unlike variables, which contain only a few words or numbers, snippets can contain any amount and any type of content—even images and tables.

Each snippet is stored in the Content Explorer's Resources\Snippets folder as a separate file with an ".flsnp" extension. This means that you can share snippets with others, receive them from others, and use them in other projects—for even more content reuse!

CONDITIONAL SNIPPETS

Just like other content, you can apply a condition tag to a snippet so that it's included or excluded from targets.

You can also create **snippet** conditions, which are condition tags you can apply to content within snippets to customize the snippet for certain topics. For more info, search on "snippet conditions" in the Flare Help system.

SNIPPET FORMATTING

Like other content, snippets can be formatted locally or by applying styles.

> *Tip* — If you need variable content that must be formatted, use a snippet instead of a variable. Variables *cannot* be formatted.

CREATING SNIPPETS

There are two ways to create snippets:

- From scratch
- From existing content

Creating snippets from scratch

Use the following procedure to create a snippet from scratch by using a template. You don't need to have a topic open to do this.

To create a snippet from scratch:

1. Select **Project → Add Snippet**. The Add New Snippet dialog opens.

2. Fill in the fields on the Add New Snippet dialog:

Option	Description
Template Folders	Folders that contain templates used to create snippets. You can select: • (Recommended) **Factory Templates** to choose a template provided with Flare, or • **My Templates** to choose one of your own snippet templates.
Templates	A list of the snippet templates in the selected template folder.

Option	Description
Preview	A preview of the selected snippet template.
Source File	The path to the selected snippet template.
Folder	(Recommended) Leave this set as Resources\Snippets.
File name	The file name for the snippet.
Stylesheet	The stylesheet to attach to the snippet.

3. Click **Add**, then **OK** to confirm the copy action.

Flare creates the snippet and copies it to the Resources\Snippets folder in your project's Content Explorer.

Snippet file

The new snippet opens in the XML Editor.

Placeholder text

4. Click in the XML Editor and type the text you want the snippet to contain. (Don't forget to replace the placeholder text.)

    Add other content as desired, such as tables, lists, and images.

5. Format the content as you would for a topic by applying styles, inserting links, etc.

6. Click **Save All** 📃 to save your work.

    You can now insert the snippet you created into any topic in your project. See "Methods for inserting snippets" on page 340.

Creating snippets from existing content

If you have content that you need to reuse in other topics, use the following procedure to turn that content into a snippet.

🔔 To create a snippet from existing content:

1. Open the topic that contains the content you want to turn into a snippet. For example, suppose you want to create a snippet for the "Important" note in the following topic.

> # Keeping your lawn healthy and green
>
> Many gardeners use chemical on their lawns regularly to keep them healthy and weed-free. You can use chemicals if you wish, but you do have other options. Next, we'll explore some natural methods of creating the beautiful lawn you desire.
>
> **Important** — Always store gardening chemicals in a cool, dry place out of the reach of children and pets.

2. Select the content you want for the snippet.

3. Select **Format → Create Snippet**. The Create Snippet dialog opens and shows the content you selected.

4. In the Snippet File field, type a name for the snippet (e.g., "ChemicalSafety Note").

> ***Important*** — Leave the Project Folder set to "Resources/Snippets."

5. To replace the selected text in the topic with the new snippet, check **Replace Source Content with the New Snippet**.

6. Click **Create**. Flare creates the snippet and copies it to the Resources\Snippets folder in your project's Content Explorer.

Snippet file

If you selected Replace Source Content … in Step 5 above, Flare replaces the source content with the new snippet. If markers are turned on, the snippet is surrounded by brackets in the topic.

Next, we'll explore some natural methods of creating the beautiful lawn you desire.

[**Important** — Always store gardening chemicals in a cool, dry place out of the reach of children and pets.]

Brackets around a snippet

You can now insert the snippet you created into any topic in your project as described next.

> *Tip* — If you have purchased MadCap Analyzer (a separate product), analyze your project for frequently used phrases. These are good candidates for snippets. Analyzer can turn those phrases into snippets and add them to your project automatically. For more information, see Analyzer's Help system.

METHODS FOR INSERTING SNIPPETS

Once you've created snippets, you can insert them into your topics in two ways:

- On a blank line
- Inside a text block

Inserting a snippet on a blank line

If you insert a snippet on a blank line in a topic, it's inserted as a block and no other content can be added to that block. If you want the snippet to be part of a text block that contains other text, then type the other text *before* inserting the snippet.

Inserting a snippet inside a text block

When snippets are inserted into a text block:

- The snippet takes on the formatting of the text block.
- If the snippet contains multiple blocks, it becomes one continuous line of text.

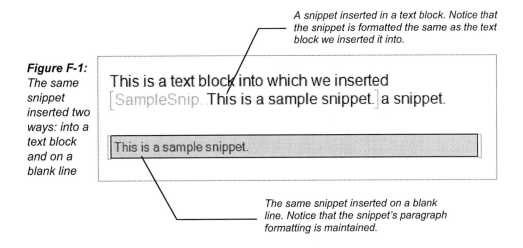

A snippet inserted in a text block. Notice that the snippet is formatted the same as the text block we inserted it into.

Figure F-1:
The same snippet inserted two ways: into a text block and on a blank line

This is a text block into which we inserted [SampleSnip. This is a sample snippet.] a snippet.

This is a sample snippet.

The same snippet inserted on a blank line. Notice that the snippet's paragraph formatting is maintained.

Figure F-2:
Snippet with multiple blocks inserted both ways

This is a text block into which we inserted [SampleSnip. This is a sample snippet.Here is a second text block in a snippet. cell 1 table text cell 2 table textcell 3 table text cell 4 table text] a snippet.

The snippet inserted on a blank line.

This is a sample snippet.

Here is a second text block in a snippet.

cell 1 table text	cell 2 table text
cell 3 table text	cell 4 table text

Procedure for inserting a snippet

Use the following procedure to insert a snippet into a topic.

To insert a snippet:

1. Open the Content Explorer.

2. Expand the **Resources** folder and then the **Snippets** sub-folder.

3. Drag-and-drop the snippet from the Content Explorer to the place in the topic where you want it to appear.

4. Click **Save All** 📑 to save your work.

> *Note* — You can also insert a snippet by selecting **Insert → Snippet** and browsing for the snippet either inside or outside of your project. For more info, search on "inserting snippets" in the Flare Help system.

CHANGING SNIPPETS

Use the following procedure to change a snippet. Flare automatically makes the changes in all topics where you've inserted the snippet.

🎁 To change a snippet:

1. To open the snippet that you want to change, do one of the following:

   - Open the Resources\Snippets folder in the Content Explorer and double-click the snippet you want to change.

   - Right-click the snippet in a topic where you've inserted it and select **Open Link**.

2. In the XML Editor, change the snippet as desired.

3. Click **Save All** 📑 to save your work.

USING VARIABLES

A **variable** holds a value that may change. Variables are useful for short pieces of content, such as a few words or a number. You can insert variables in topics, master pages, page layout frames, and snippets—in short, wherever you create content.

> *Note* — You can also add variables to TOC entries, browse sequence entries, and links by adding the variable syntax manually, but this is an advanced feature beyond the scope of this book. If interested, search on "About Variables" in the Flare Help system.

By changing the value of a variable *before* building output, you can vary the output.

AN EXAMPLE

Suppose you want to place a version number in several places in your output. To do so, you'd create a variable for version number, give it a value, and insert it wherever you want it used.

Later, if the version number changes, you just update the variable. When you build your output, the new value is automatically used wherever you inserted the variable.

> **Note** — You can also update the value of a variable for one target only, without changing the value used for all other targets.

CONDITIONAL VARIABLES

Just like other content, you can apply a condition tag to a variable so that it's included or excluded from targets.

VARIABLE FORMATTING

Variable content *cannot* be formatted, either locally or with styles.

VARIABLE SETS

Flare stores variables in sets, and each set can contain many variables. Out-of-the-box, Flare includes three variable sets:

- Heading
- MyVariables
- System

> **Important** — You can insert variables from all three sets, but you can change only "MyVariables" by adding more variables to it or by changing its variables. One variable set might be adequate for you, but you can add more variable sets if desired. Search on "variable sets" and see "Adding Variable Sets To Projects" in the Flare Help system.

A variable has two main parts—a *name* and a *definition*. (The comment is optional.)

The variable set you can customize (MyVariables)

Change the definitions or delete these variables provided by MadCap Software.

Figure F-3: *Variables dialog*

Types of Variables

Flare contains these kinds of variables:

- **User-defined**, which are the ones you add to the MyVariables set or to another variable set that you create.

- **System**, which includes variables such as page number, date, and time.

- **Heading**, which are heading styles h1 through h6 (useful for displaying heading text in running headers and footers in print output).

> **Note**— If you create print output in PDF, XPS, or XHTML format, you can use heading variables to show headings and terms in the glossary and index.

INSERTING VARIABLES

Use the following procedure to insert a variable into a topic.

 To insert a variable:

1. Open the topic you want to insert a variable into.

2. Place your cursor where you want to insert a variable.

3. Select **Insert → Variable**. The Variables dialog opens (Figure F-3).

4. Select the desired variable set (initially Heading, MyVariables, and System). The set's variables are shown on the right.

5. Select the variable you want to insert. (You might need to scroll through the list.)

6. Click **OK**. The variable is added to the topic. If markers are turned on, you'll see brackets around the variable. If variable names are turned on, you'll also see the variable name.

Variable name ⎯⎯⎯⎯⎯⎯⎯⎯⎯⎯⎯⎯⎯⎯ Value

For help, call ⟦ PhoneNumb... 858 123 4567 ⟧

If markers are *not* turned on, you'll see only the variable's value.

For help, call 858 123 4567

> *Tip* — To turn on markers, click the arrow to the right of **Toggle show tags** ⟨t⟩ ▾ in the XML Editor toolbar, and select **Show Markers**. To turn on variable names, click **Show Variable Names**.

7. Click **Save All** 💾 to save your work.

Highlighting Variables

When you're viewing content, you can easily distinguish variables from other content if variable highlighting is turned on.

Figure F-4:
Variable
highlighting
turned on

For help, call 858 123 4567

 To toggle highlighting on or off:

- Select **View → Show → Highlight Variables**.

Adding and Changing Variables

You can do any of the following in your own variable sets:

- Add new variables

- Rename variables

- Change a variable's value (its "definition")

- Delete a variable from the set

- Add comments

If you change a variable's value after inserting the variable into topics, Flare automatically changes the result in those topics.

 To change a variable:

1. Open the Project Organizer.

2. Expand the **Variables** folder.

    > **Note** — Only user-defined variable sets are listed, since you cannot change the System or Heading variable sets.

3. Double-click the variable set you want to change, such as MyVariables. The VariableSet Editor opens.

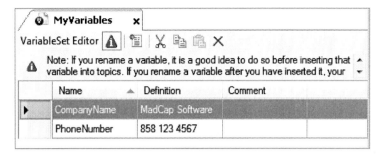

4. Add or change variables as described in this table:

To ...	Do this ...
Add a new variable	<ul><li>In the VariableSet Editor's toolbar, click **New item** . A new row appears, and Flare assigns a temporary name.</li><li>To change the name, click it, press **F2**, and type a new name.</li><li>To enter a value, click in the Definition field, press **F2**, and type the value.</li></ul>
Rename a variable	<ul><li>Click the name and press **F2**.</li><li>Type the new name.</li></ul>
Change a variable's value	<ul><li>Click in the Definition column for the variable you want to change and press **F2**.</li><li>Type the new value and click **OK**.</li></ul>
Add a comment	<ul><li>Click in the variable's Comment field.</li><li>Press **F2** and type a comment. (Comments don't appear in the output.)</li></ul>

5. Click **Save All** to save your work.

Appendix G:
The Next Step

In this chapter …
- ➤ Advanced features to explore
- ➤ Additional features when working with styles

Now it's up to you

At this point, you've learned enough about Flare to complete your first project, and you might want to know a bit about which features to check out next.

Flare is a powerful tool for topic-based authoring, with many options to explore. Table G-1 gives you a brief description of some of the features you might want to learn about on your own. Consult the Flare Help system for detailed information.

Table G-1: Flare features to explore

With this feature ...	You can ...
Global project linking	▪ Import content and files from one project into another. ▪ Maintain the content in the original (source) project and reuse it in another.
Topic review and contribution	▪ Email topics to request feedback and changes. **Note** — Reviewers can add annotations or change topics using MadCap X-Edit or X-Edit Review and return comments to you. ▪ Accept reviewers' comments and add them to the source file. ▪ Create templates for others to use with X-Edit or X-Edit Contribute. ▪ Add topics created by others to your project.
Annotations	▪ Insert comments and notes in topics. ▪ Accept annotations made by others into your project's source file.
Topic element lock	▪ Prevent editing to areas in your topics, such as specific paragraphs. (Locked areas appear gray, which can be turned on or off as you work.) ▪ Allow full access to topics after a review.
Footnotes	▪ Add footnotes to your topics.

Table G-1:
(Cont.)

With this feature ...	You can ...
Content auto-numbering	▪ Number content automatically (a more advanced method of creating numbered lists).
Movies	▪ Launch MadCap Mimic right from Flare. ▪ Add links to MadCap Mimic movies. ▪ Change and preview movies.
Project properties	▪ Use the Project Properties dialog to specify the project's master TOC, master stylesheet, master page layout, spell-check language and source control application (**Project → Project Properties**).
Auto-save (version 4.2 and up)	▪ Use the Options dialog to automatically save all open files according to a specified time interval (**Tools → Options**).
Window, topic and editor manipulation	▪ Position topics side-by-side by floating them (useful if you use dual monitors). ▪ Float windows and editors to move them where you need them. ▪ Attach windows to the sides, top, or bottom of the workspace by docking them. ▪ Move a window to the middle pane (right-click the title bar of the window and select **Send To Main Dock**).
Dialog and drop-down menu resizing	▪ Resize all dialogs and drop-down menus by clicking and dragging their edges.
Custom layouts	▪ Open and position Flare windows per your needs. Then save the layout as a configuration. ▪ Create multiple configurations for different needs.
Text boxes	▪ Insert a box into a topic and add content to it. ▪ Position a text box as desired.
Glossary headings	▪ Define if headings will appear at the top of each glossary section (by using a glossary proxy). ▪ Change the appearance of glossary headings (by using the div.GlossaryPageHeading style class in your stylesheet).

Table G-1:
(Cont.)

With this feature ...	You can ...
Object positioning	• Position objects, such as images and text boxes, exactly where you want them (object positioning must be enabled).
Hyphenation (print output)	• Specify if hyphens will be used at the end of lines.
Mini-TOCs (print output)	• Create mini-TOCs for chapters (by inserting a mini-TOC proxy into each topic that begins a chapter).
"List of" proxy	• Create a linked list of various types of elements in your output, such as tables or images.
Page and column break icons (Print Layout mode)	• Determine where page / column breaks or widow / orphan control have forced a paragraph to move to another page (icons appear in the text margins). • Open the paragraph properties (by clicking a page or column break icon).
Elimination of short lines	• Widen or narrow the last line of a paragraph when it is only a certain number of characters long.
Page breaks on table rows	• Break pages on table rows (by specifying the "page-break-inside" setting on the <tr> style tag used for table rows).
Widows and orphans	• Define widow and orphan settings locally and in a style.
Advanced index options	• Add index terms automatically rather than inserting index markers manually. • Exclude index entries from searches (by default, index entries are included in searches). • Link index entries to other index entries ("see" and "see also" links). • Display index entries with multiple pages in a range, such as 3-5.
Italics spacing	• Increase the space between an italicized word and a non-italicized word.

Table G-1: (Cont.)	With this feature ...	You can ...
	File name conversion to lowercase (online output)	▪ Convert output file names and folders to lowercase letters (useful in UNIX environments).
	Batch processing / command line compilation	▪ Use your operating system's command line to build output without ever opening Flare. ▪ Build output using one or more targets in a single batch.
	Languages	▪ Enable users to view DotNet Help in a variety of available languages by using the MadCap Help Viewer. ▪ Customize skins in other languages for WebHelp, WebHelp Plus, or WebHelp AIR.
	MadCap news **☺ MadCap News Available!**	▪ View news from MadCap Software.
	Web-safe image output	▪ Convert non–web-safe image formats to web-safe formats when you build online output (by using the Advanced tab of the Target Editor). Original image file formats are used when you build print output.

ADDITIONAL FEATURES WHEN WORKING WITH STYLES

In addition to *applying* styles as described in this book, you can:

▪ Create topic stylesheets.

▪ Create table stylesheets.

▪ Add and change styles in both table and topic stylesheets.

▪ Apply a style using the Floating Style Picker (rather than choosing a style in the Text Format toolbar or Styles window). To use the Style Picker, click in the desired content, press **CTRL + SHIFT + H**, choose a style and press **ENTER**.

▪ Hide styles in a stylesheet (to reduce the number of styles available). Styles are not deleted, but are simply disabled.

- Apply master stylesheets to a project and/or target. When applied to a project, the styles are available for all project content. When applied to a target, the styles are available for all target content.

> **Note** — If you use one master stylesheet for a project and another for a target, the stylesheet applied to the target will take precedence.

Index

How to Order

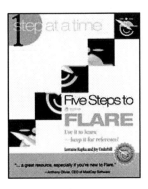

To order additional copies of *Five Steps to MadCap Flare*, contact Windsor Media Enterprises, LLC, at:

WWW.WMEBOOKS.COM
1-877-947-BOOK (2665)

Ask for it at your local bookstore by title, author name, or:

ISBN-10: 1-934229-10-5
ISBN-13: 978-1-934229-10-1

For information about quantity purchases, discounts, and special programs, please contact:

Special Book Orders
Windsor Media Enterprises, LLC
282 Ballad Avenue
Rochester, NY 14626
info@wmebooks.com

Visit the authors at:

WWW.NORTHCOASTWRITERS.COM